STATE OF ILLINOIS
DEPARTMENT OF PUBLIC WORKS AND BUILDINGS
DIVISION OF HIGHWAYS

BULLETIN NO. 16

I0117040

Manual on Road Construction

For

Resident Engineers and Inspectors

Prepared by

B. H. PIEPMEIER,

Engineer of Construction, Division of Highways
LEN SMALL, *Governor*
C. R. MILLER, *Director*
THOMAS G. VENNUM, *Assistant Director*
S. E. BRADT, *Superintendent of Highways*
CLIFFORD OLDER, *Chief Highway Engineer*

BUREAU CHIEFS

F. T. SHEETS, *Engineer of Design*
B. H. PIEPMEIER, *Engineer of Construction*
FRED TARRANT, *Engineer of Maintenance*
H. F. CLEMMER, *Engineer of Tests*
D. H. CORNELL, *Superintendent of Machinery*
J. M. McCOY, *Chief Clerk*

SPRINGFIELD, ILLINOIS
April, 1921

CONTENTS.

	Para-graph.	Page.
eface		7
ganization		9
Bureau chiefs	1	9
District engineers	2	9
Assistant engineers, junior engineers and highway inspectors	3	9
County superintendent of highways	4	9
Township and district commissioners	5	9
ities of resident engineers and inspectors—		
Sizing up job	6	9
Acquaintance and publicity	7	10
Locating resident headquarters	8	10
Remaining on job	9	10
Correspondence	10	10
Transportation to and from work	11	11
Field equipment	12	11
Examination of plans and specifications	13	12
Locating B. M.'s	14	12
Locating balance points	15	12
Right-of-way	16	12
Corner Stones	17	13
Grading stakes	18	13
Earth shrinkage	19	14
Slope stakes	20	14
Super-elevating curves	21	14
Final grade stakes	22	14
Contractor's equipment and methods	23	15
Giving instructions	24	15
aily routine of engineers in charge of road construction	25	15
eports	26	17
Weekly reports	27	17
Records	28	17
Cost records	29	17
Records of underground work	30	18
Record of bridge piling	31	18
Extra work	32	18
'ater supply—		
Quantity and quality	33	19
Deep wells and reservoirs	34	19
Pipe line	35	19
Pipe connections	36	20
Pump	37	20
oad bed—		
Subgrade	38	20
Scarifying and shaping	39	21
Wetting subgrade	40	21
Rolling subgrade	41	22
Unrolled subgrade	42	23
Driving on subgrade	43	23
Porous materials for subgrade	44	23
Tiling subgrade	45	23
Oiling subgrade	46	23

CONTENTS—Continued.

	Para-graph.	P
Frozen subgrade	47	
Materials on subgrade	48	
Backfilling trenches and bridge abutments	49	
Laying pavement—		
Concrete mixer	50	
Timing devices	51	
Charging mixer	52	
Installation of corrugated joints	53	
Tie bars	54	
Subgrade templates	55	
Header boards	56	
Noon day construction joints	57	
Construction joints	58	
Late fall construction	59	
One-half of pavement built at a time	60	
Side forms for pavements	61	
Proportioning aggregates and cement	62	
Combination truck and industrial railroad delivery	63	
Team delivery to mixer	64	
Proportioning materials in batch boxes	65	
Cement—		
Protecting cement in transit to mixer	66	
Bulk cement	67	
Cement in sacks	68	
Damaged cement	69	
Cement records and reports	70	
Cleaning cement sacks	71	
Storing cement	72	
Cement tests	73	
Borrowing or buying cement	74	
Materials—		
Material tests	75	
Storing material	76	
Central mixing plants	77	
Hauling mixed concrete	78	
Consistency of mixed concrete	79	
Finishing mixed concrete	80	
Finishing concrete pavements—		
Finishing machine	81	
Checking finished surface	82	
Overtamping surface	83	
Final finish	84	
Hand roller and belt	85	
Finishing curves	86	
Use of 10-foot straight edge	87	
Character of finished pavement	88	
Special sections—		
Curb and gutter sections	89	
Curb and gutter turnouts	90	
Grate bars	91	
Gutter sections	92	
Curing	93	
Ponding method of curing	94	
Use of straw for curing	95	
Earth covering	96	
Protecting pavement by use of frames and canvas	97	
Experimental methods of curing pavements	98	
Fall and spring curing	99	
Protecting surface in freezing weather	100	
Preventing concrete from freezing	101	
Monolithic brick pavements	102	

CONTENTS—Concluded.

	Paragraph.	Page.
Finishing base course	103	48
Finishing brick surface	104	49
Grouting brick surface	105	49
Uniform surface	106	50
Curing	107	50
Bituminous filled brick construction—		
Concrete base	108	50
Curing base	109	50
Gravel and macadam bases	110	50
Cushion	111	50
Laying and rolling brick	112	51
Bituminous filler	113	51
Curing surface	114	51
Bituminous concrete pavements—		
Finishing base	115	51
Curing	116	52
Concrete curb	117	52
Binder and wearing courses	118	52
Gravel roads	119	53
Trench and feather-edge construction	120	53
Crown	121	54
Macadam roads	122	54
Crown	123	55
Bituminous macadam roads	124	55
Surface treatment	125	55
Surface treating gravel roads	126	56
Earth roads	127	56
Grading machinery	128	57
Earth road maintenance	129	57
Oiled earth roads	130	57
Shoulders and side ditches—		
Cross sections	131	58
Side ditches	132	58
Hand work	133	58
Finishing shoulders	134	59
Entrance culverts	135	59
Acceptance of work	136	59
Completing details of work	137	59
Certified checks	138	60
Partial acceptance	139	60
Payment estimates	140	60
Payment for materials	141	61
Freight increase and reductions	142	62
Semi-final estimates	143	62
Affidavit	144	62
Detour and barricade signs	145	68
Warning sign	146	68
Road closed	147	68
Detour signs	148	68
Purchasing and erecting	149	68
Maintenance of signs	150	68
Maintenance of detour road	151	69
Barricades	152	69

LIST OF ILLUSTRATIONS.

Fig.
No.   Pa

1. Temporary reservoir adjacent to deep well to hold surplus water during paving operations
2. Preparing subgrade in advance of a paving mixer.....................................
3. Horse roller coupled to caterpillar tractor and used for rolling subgrade..............
4. Material stored at intervals of 600 feet along the side of the road. Short industrial
   track delivers material from storage piles to paving mixer.........................
5. One and one-half ton pneumatic tired truck delivering mixed concrete from central
   plant to road ....
6. Aggregate stored on top of a tunnel permits a large storage of material and easy
   method of filling batch boxes on industrial railroad equipment.....................
7. Concrete pavement cured by ponding method. Note tunnel and material yard and
   cement storage bins in background..
8. Material plant for central proportioning batch boxes for industrial railroad delivery.....
9. Transfer station for material boxes from trucks to industrial cars. Industrial cars
   deliver materials to paving mixer about one mile ahead............................
10. One-ton truck loaded with mixed concrete being turned on subgrade...............
11. Central mixing plant ....
12. Porous spots in concrete surface can be avoided if a small amount of concrete is
    kept in advance of the templet when the finishing machine is moved forward......
13. Ten-foot straight edge shows up a depression of three-fourths inch in the finished
    surface ....
14. Slope-wall construction to protect road from excessive erosion......................
15. Curb and gutter outlet at bottom of steep grade...................................
16. Gutter section on steep grade and through a heavy cut.............................
17. Curb and gutter construction on steep grades and through heavy cuts................
18. Canvas covering on newly laid concrete pavement to protect it from sun and wind.
    Canvas should be kept wet when weather is extremely hot.........................
19. Canvas covered frames used to cover a concrete road immediately behind the paving
    mixer ....
20. Monolithic brick road showing concrete base and brick surface being finished with
    a mechanical tamping and finishing machine......................................
21. Corrugated hand roller used to roughen concrete surface for a bituminous concrete
    pavement ....
22. Dumping, spreading, and rolling bituminous concrete on a concrete base.............
23. Trench method of constructing macadam or gravel roads............................
24. Gravel road constructed by the feather-edge method................................
25. Method used for distributing bituminous material for surface treatment of macadam
    and gravel roads or for oiling earth roads.......................................
26. Condition of macadam surface after first application of one and one-half to two gallons
    per square yard of bituminous material is applied. This treatment to be followed
    with stone chips or torpedo gravel then one-half to three-fourths gallon per square
    yard and another covering of stone chips or gravel...............................
27. Well graded and oiled earth road..
28. Showing well shaped shoulder and side ditch.......................................
29. Itemized material statement and affidavit..
30. Memorandum of cars received..
31. Excess freight and war tax affidavit...
32. Release for semi-final estimate ....
33. Contractor's affidavit ....
34. Suggested form of bill for extra work...
35. Road closed sign showing engineer's notations.....................................
36. Standard warning sign for barricades..
37. Standard detour sign showing engineer's notations before erecting..................
38. Map showing positions of barricade and detour sign................................

PREFACE.

The purpose of this bulletin is to set forth briefly the requirements of the Department of Public Works and Buildings, in the construction of various types of roads. It must be understood that all preliminary work in the location of right-of-way, surveys, plans and specifications, regardless of the time or talent employed in the preparation of the work, may be useless if the construction is not intelligently and fairly executed. During the next ten years it is estimated that one hundred million dollars will be spent for road improvement in Illinois. It is very important, therefore, that all work be done in accordance with approved principles and under intelligent supervision in order that the burden imposed by future maintenance may be reduced to a minimum.

No set of rules and no set of specifications can be written to cover completely all conditions which may arise. Experience, judgment, and integrity in carrying out the requirements of the specifications must dictate the answer to many doubtful questions that may arise in the construction of the work.

It is hoped, therefore, that this bulletin may offer suggestions that will aid both the engineer and the contractor in the successful completion of his work.

ORGANIZATION.

The purpose of the revised road and bridge law is to provide a competent organization for the efficient handling of all road and bridge work in the State. Under the Civil Administrative Code the Director of the Department of Public Works and Buildings directs the work of the Division of Highways. The Superintendent and Chief Highway Engineer of the Division of Highways in conjunction with the Director and the Board of Highway Advisors determine the location and direct the design, construction, and maintenance of all State road and bridge work.

All of the above named officials are appointed by the Governor. All other employes connected with the Division of Highways are under Civil Service.

1. *Bureau Chiefs.* For convenience and efficiency, the work of the Division is administered through six Bureaus; namely, the Bureau of Design, Bureau of Construction, Bureau of Maintenance, Bureau of Tests, Bureau of Machinery, and Bureau of Audits. All matters according to the class of work involved should be referred to the bureau in charge of the particular work in question.

2. *District Engineers.* To facilitate field work, nine geographical districts have been established with a district engineer in charge of each district. They represent the State in all field work pertaining to road and bridge construction and maintenance in their respective districts and report directly to the bureau chief according to the nature of the work under consideration.

3. *Assistant Engineers, Junior Engineers and Highway Inspectors.* These men are placed on one or more sections of road and bridge construction and are responsible to the district engineer for the execution of the work in accordance with the plans and specifications.

4. *County Superintendents of Highways.* The county superintendents of Highways direct all county and township work and are subject to the rules and regulations of the State Division of Highways. Matters which they wish to take up with the Department should be handled through their district engineer.

5. *Township and District Commissioners.* These officials have immediate charge of all work within their respective townships or road districts subject to the approval of the county superintendent of highways.

DUTIES OF RESIDENT ENGINEERS AND INSPECTORS.

6. *Sizing up Job.* In the execution of any piece of work it is essential that proper preparation be made by both the inspector or engineer in charge and the contractor before any extensive expendi-

ture of time or money is made. When work is once started th
money allotted or available for its execution is usually spent in
comparatively short time. The contractor and engineer, therefore
should both have a very complete understanding of the plans an
specifications and of all conditions surrounding or affecting the wor
before active construction begins. Considerable lost time, effort, an
money are usually the result of misunderstanding and lack of know
ledge of the conditions affecting the work. The successful enginee
or contractor will therefore spend considerable time in sizing up th
job in all of its details before starting construction.

7. *Acquaintance and Publicity.* The resident engineer or in
spector, after sizing up the job, should make a special effort to be
come acquainted with the leading men in the community. It
especially important that you call upon the local newspapers and giv
them complete information in regard to your mission. You shoul
also make a special effort to keep them informed at least once eac
week in regard to the progress of the work and any other items o
news in connection with the construction that will be of genera
interest to the public. In giving out information of this kind, kee
in mind that you are an employee of the State and all statements mac
should reflect the attitude of the State and not your personal idea
concerning the work in question.

8. *Locating Resident Headquarters.* When assigned to a res
dent job, *advise the telephone and telegraph offices immediately whei
you may be located.* You will make a special effort to locate you
lodging headquarters at a place where you may be reached readily l
telephone or telegram and by anyone who will naturally wish to ca
upon you for information relating to the work. You will also try t
locate as near to your work as possible or at a place convenient fo
transportation to and from the job. A private rooming house w
give you a much better rate and will usually prove more satisfactor
than the average hotel. If necessary to stay at a hotel, reduce
weekly rates should be secured. You will not always be able to s
cure meals at a private boarding house on account of your irregula
hours during the construction season. It may be necessary, therefor
for you to plan for your meals at restaurants and hotels. Keep
mind that inspection costs shall be kept as low as possible consister
with reasonably good living conditions.

9. *Remaining on the Job.* You are expected to be on the jo
at all times while construction operations are in progress. If abs
lutely necessary to be off the job, secure permit from your distri
engineer and then choose a time when the least important operatio
are under way. When important construction operations are in pr
gress, watch every detail regardless of the time or hours it may tak
The Department expects you to watch all phases of the work.
this requires more time than you are physically able to give to it, th
Department will furnish you additional help.

10. *Correspondence.* All correspondence relating to your wo1
shall be addressed to your district engineer. It shall be identified l

placing at the top of each letter the subject matter and the section, county, and project or route; e. g. "Cement, Sec. I, Madison Co., Project 8" or "Estimate, Sec. II, Greene Co., S. A." Do not refer to more than one section or main subject in any one letter.

11. *Transportation to and from Work.* When a State automobile is assigned to you, you will be held responsible for its safe keeping and for its being in reasonably good running condition at all times. Small ordinary repairs shall be made promptly. The district engineer shall be consulted before extensive repairs or overhauling are authorized. Except in emergencies, tubes and casings will be furnished from the district office and you should request spare tires a sufficient time in advance of your needs to make it possible for them to be secured from the superintendent of machinery at Springfield. In purchasing gasoline, oil, and other automobile supplies, receipted bills shall be obtained and submitted to the district office at the time you submit your expense account. They shall, however, be kept and listed separate from your expense account.

After an automobile is assigned to you it shall be used exclusively for State business. If it is found you are using a State car for pleasure and private purposes, it will be evidence that you do not respect the rules of the Department and will be sufficient grounds for dismissal from the service.

12. *Field Equipment.* Resident Engineers, before leaving the district office should generally provide themselves with the following supplies and equipment:

Letter heads, envelopes, postage
Pencils and lumber crayon
Field book, Cost record book
Itemized expense book
Sub-voucher blanks
Tax exemption certificates
Daily Report Cards
Weekly progress report blanks
Weekly cement report cards
Set of Plans of the road to be improved
Transit, tripods, plumb-bob and reading glass.
Level rod, range pole
100 ft. engineer's steel tape
50 ft. steel tape
50 ft. metallic tape
Straight edge
Automobile
2 spare casings
2 spare inner tubes
Equipment and tools.

When additional supplies are needed, make request by letter to the district engineer.

All survey instruments, tapes, chains, rods, etc. when taken from the office are charged to your account and the department numbers

recorded. No equipment shall be taken out of the office witho
a record being made of the charge.

Transits and levels should be removed from the tripods and ke
in the box at night and when not in use they should be left in a sa
place, preferably in your own room. The practice of leaving the i
strument on the tripod and setting it in a farm yard, out building,
residence is carelessness. Tapes and chains should be cleaned and oile
occasionally to prevent rusting and rods should be handled, carried at
shipped in a manner that will preserve the paint and the numera
Any employee of ordinary engineering training will appreciate tl
value of such equipment and will try to preserve it accordingly.

13. *Examination of Plans and Specifications.* You will secu
from your district engineer a complete set of the plans and specific
tions for the work to which you have been assigned. You will th
take the plans into the field and go over all parts of the work no
ing in your permanent memorandum book items which are in que
tion or which you think should be taken up with your district eng
neer. Make sure that you fully understand all of the requiremen
of the plans and specifications. If there are any discrepancies
points which are not clear, do not hesitate to make a memorandu
of them and get into communication immediately with your distri
engineer. Make a special effort to go over all details of the pla
and specifications with the contractor or superintendent in charge
the work. If there are any points which are not entirely clear
the contractor, it is necessary to explain them and to reach son
agreement concerning the execution of the work before active co
struction is begun.

14. *Locating B. M.'s.* Before doing any survey work, you w
check your transit and level for adjustments. You will then loca
on the ground all B. M. and P. I. which are referred to on the pla
and check them carefully to make sure they agree with the not
tions on the plans. When checking B. M. and P. I., you will arrang
to set other B. M. at intervening points so that you will have a B.
about every one thousand feet and one at each cross road culver
Special care should be taken to locate B. M. and P. I. so that th
will not be disturbed by grading operations.

15. *Locating Balance Points.* Before any grading is done yo
will mark by means of a pole or otherwise all balance points throug
out the length of the road. This is very necessary for the contract
so that he may move the earth in the right direction thereby elimina
ing future trouble with regard to shortage or surplus of earth wh
completing the work.

Before any grading or bridge work is done you will ascerta
the amount of road that will have to be detoured by traffic and th
arrange to erect the necessary detour signs in accordance with i
structions found in paragraphs 145 to 151.

16. *Right-of-Way.* Before grading is started you will chec
the right-of-way lines of the entire road. Where additional right-o
way has been secured you will set stakes for the new right-of-wz

fence line and notify the property owner in writing to remove the fence at least fifteen days in advance of the time you expect to disturb the road at that particular point. You will also communicate with your district engineer in regard to all poles or other obstructions within the limits of the graded roadway so that he may notify the utility companies in writing to clear the right-of-way. Utility companies should be notified a sufficient time in advance of construction work to enable them to have the right-of-way cleared.

17. *Corner Stones.* Before any grading operations have been started, you will arrange to locate if possible all permanent survey monuments such as right-of-way and section corner stones. The section corner stones are permanent points and should in no case be disturbed without proper record being taken of their exact location in order that the monument may be re-established in the finished work. If you are not able to locate section corner stones you will get into communication with the county surveyor or county superintendent of highways who will assist you in the location of the monuments. Any expense incurred by the county surveyor in locating section corner stones will be borne by the State. It will be your duty, however, to reference the monuments in such a manner that they can be re-established in the finished work. In case the pavement covers the corner stone, a cast iron plug six inches square and three inches thick with a cross upon its face shall be accurately set in the surface of the finished pavement and such information given to the county surveyor for his permanent record.

18. *Grading Stakes.* Grading stakes will be furnished by the contractor and should ordinarily be set in accordance with his wishes. In general, they will be set at intervals of one hundred feet along the fence line and the proper cut and fill for the finished pavement indicated on them. Ordinarily stakes on one side of the road will be sufficient for the preliminary grading work. In some instances, however, the contractor will wish stakes on both fence lines so that he may "T" across the road for his intermediate points. Extreme care should be exercised in locating and marking preliminary stakes so that they will not be disturbed, and so that they will contain the proper information in regard to the grade line to be established. Changing grade stakes frequently results in considerable delay and expense to the contractor. In addition to the grade stakes set along the property line, the contractor will usually wish a line stake in the center of his road at intervals of 300 or 400 feet.

On curves it will be necessary to set stakes at intervals of 25 to 50 feet on both sides of the road, preferably about fifteen feet from the center line of the pavement so that the grading foreman may establish the proper super-elevation at the time the grading work is being done. Grade stakes in general should show the cut or fill to the finished pavement and not to the subgrade. This would not be true with an earth grading section, however, as the stakes in this case would show the finished grade of the earth work.

19. *Earth Shrinkage.* In no case should grade stakes show th
shrinkage that should be provided in fill sections. Shrinkage wi
vary from 10 to 35 per cent depending upon the character of the so
and the way the fills are made. The engineer shall therefore sho'
the finished grade line elevation and require the contractor to allo'
sufficient excess of material to provide for the shrinkage. In genera
where earth grading will average from 2000 to 3000 cubic yards pe
mile of road, 25 to 35 per cent should be allowed in cut over fill t
provide for waste and shrinkage. On work where grading will aver
age from 3000 to 8000 cubic yards per mile of road, 15 to 25 per cei
should be allowed in cut over fill. On grading that will average fror
8000 to 12000 cubic yards per mile, 10 to 18 per cent should be a
lowed for cut over fill. If the excavated material is sandy, 7 to 1
per cent of cut over fill will usually provide for the shrinkage.
should be kept in mind that excavation in rock will swell from 5 to 2
per cent over the fill section.

The above figures are only approximate and will vary materiall
with the character of the soil and the methods used by the contracte
in making the fills.

20. *Slope Stakes.* In all cuts and fills exceeding three fee
stakes shall be set at the toe of the slope. The location of these stake
shall be computed from actual instrument readings at the point whei
the stake is set, and should be accurate to the nearest tenth of a foo
The stake shall indicate the cut or fill for the finished grade disri
garding the shrinkage.

21. *Superelevating Curves.* All curves shall be staked in suc
a manner that the proper superelevation will be made when the roa
is graded. Unless otherwise noted on the plans the superelevatio
will commence 150 feet from the P. C. and attain the maximum ;
the P. C. The center line of the pavement shall follow the true grac
as shown on the plans. The inside of the curve shall be depressed on
half of the amount of the superelevation and the outside of the cury
raised one-half of the amount of the superelevation. Superelevation should extend from shoulder line to shoulder line.

22. *Final Grade Stakes.* Final grade stakes should be set tri
to line and grade at intervals of 50 to 100 feet on both sides of tl
center line of the pavement and usually about two feet from its edg
In many instances one line of stakes is sufficient as a good form sette
can transfer the grades to the form on the opposite side of the roa
with an ordinary carpenter's level.

On horizontal and vertical curves, finished grade stakes shoul
be set at intervals of 25 feet. On tangents where there are no vertic;
curves, the grade stakes should be set by establishing points at inte·
vals of 400 or 500 feet and then locating all intermediate grade stake
by the shooting method. On curves a chalk line should be strung o
all stakes established and a careful inspection of the alignment an
grade made with the eye. If the alignment and grade does not loo
right, it probably is wrong and should be checked carefully with tl
instrument, or the stakes should be shifted by eye so that the pave

ment will fit the ground and give the proper appearance. Make it a rule to reference as many stakes on the job as possible as a great many of them will be disturbed by construction operations and you may be called upon frequently by the contractor to establish the grade when in many cases you have only a limited amount of time. Use your eye frequently in checking stakes set with an instrument. This will often catch errors and relieve you of embarrassment and save the contractor delay and expense.

23. *Contractor's Equipment and Methods.* Do not discuss promiscuously with the general public the methods of the contractor or the equipment which he is using on the job. You should concern yourself with the quality of the work produced and not so much with the methods of the contractor.

24. *Giving Instructions.* You should refrain from issuing orders or giving instructions to individuals on contract work. The contractor's foreman or superintendent on the work should be respected and all instructions to the men issued through him. If he does not carry out your instructions the matter should be taken up with the contractor, and then if no improvement is made, it should be reported to your district engineer.

DAILY ROUTINE OF ENGINEERS IN CHARGE OF ROAD CONSTRUCTION.

25. The following daily routine of an engineer in charge of road inspection work is given merely as a suggestion that he may not overlook some of the important details that arise on practically every section of work. No set of rules or specifications can be written to cover completely all conditions which may be encountered as the routine of inspections will vary considerably with different jobs. Experience and good judgment must dictate your actions on construction work. The following routine, however, shows a few of the fundamental duties of the engineer and should be followed as a general guide in the inspection of road work.

1. Check cars received at the unloading station.

2. See that header board at the close of the previous day's work is removed.

3. See that subgrade is cleaned up behind the mixer.

4. *Check surface of pavement with a ten-foot straight edge* adjacent to the construction joint.

5. See that sufficient grade stakes are set for the pavement and the rough grading.

6. Check alignment of forms with the eye.

7. See that all side forms have a substantial bearing and have been oiled.

8. Check subgrade in advance of the mixer.

9. Walk back over the past two weeks' work to see that it is being cured properly. Set some form of a marker at the end of the

two weeks' work. This will serve as a guide to the individual wh
is looking after the curing of the pavement.

10. Examine the material arriving on the job.

11. Check quantity of material in batches and amount o
cement used.

12. See that new concrete adjacent to the construction joint ha
been properly edged and finished, *and check with a 10-foot straigh
edge*. I insist upon a perfect joint.

13. Check alignment and grade of finished pavement.

14. *Use a 10-foot straight edge* on forms and finished pavemen

15. Check revolutions and time the mixer is mixing concrete.

16. Check consistency of concrete.

17. See that the tamping machine is doing its work.

18. Record number of men working on subgrade, forms aroun
mixer, finishing, curing, etc.

19. Check up work being done on culverts and bridges in ad
vance of the paving work.

20. See that all the previous day's work has been covered an
sprinkled or is being cured properly.

21. Check alignment of forms and finish of pavement complete
during the day. *Use a 10-foot straight edge.*

22. Check position of reinforcing steel in pavement.

23. See that pavement has been properly edged.

24. See that all concrete is thoroughly spaded and that there ar
no stone pockets in the road or adjacent to the forms.

25. Measure distance between the construction joint and noo
day header board.

26. Check total number of batches or sacks used during th
morning's work.

27. See that the noon day header board is properly placed an
that the reinforcing steel is in place.

Afternoon. Repeat all operations in afternoon except thos
designated in paragraphs 1, 9, 19, and 23, and in addition look afte
the following items of work.

28. Check shoulder and ditch work being done on finished pave
ment.

29. See that pavement is cleaned after the two weeks' perio
of curing.

30. See that new pavement is being covered with frames o
convas.

31. See, if possible, that all barricades and detours are in plac
before leaving work. Inspect all detours and signs at least once eac
week.

32. Check cost items on all force account work with the super
intendent or foreman.

33. Measure total pavement laid during the day and check cement sacks used.

34. Make daily reports and record all data necessary for weekly reports.

REPORTS.

26. Daily reports shall be made to your district engineer on blank cards furnished for this purpose. These reports shall give a brief record of the work done and should ordinarily include a report of materials received, grading, work done on bridges and culverts, pavement laid, weather conditions, etc. One report shall be made for each mixer in operation on the job.

27. *Weekly Reports.* Weekly reports shall be made promptly after the close of the work Thursday night. They should be in the district office by Saturday and in the Springfield office by Monday. On Federal Aid work they shall be mailed to the district office in triplicate so that one copy may go to the Federal district engineer, one may be retained by the district engineer and one sent to the Springfield office. If you do not keep a permanent record in your notebook of the progress of your work, you shall keep a copy of all weekly reports for future reference. The weekly report is the most important of all the reports you make concerning your work. For this reason, therefore, the man supervising your duties will judge your work largely by the reports you make. All of the blank spaces provided on the report blanks shall be filled out. Statistics in the main office are kept from weekly reports sent in by field men. You will therefore indicate on the report the cause for no work being done or for delays. You will also indicate under the item "Feet Laid Per Day" whether one or two gangs were working and the number of mixers used during each day pavement was laid.

28. *Records.* The Department will furnish all resident engineers and inspectors with a field notebook in the form of a survey book or construction record book for the purpose of keeping a complete record of all operations in connection with the execution of the work to which you have been assigned. The notebook is the property of the State and when the job is completed or when the book is filled should be filed with your district engineer as a record of the work done by you in connection with the construction of the road or bridge. The book shall also contain your name and address and the address of the district office so that in case of loss it may be returned to the proper owner. It shall be made up in such a manner that it will furnish you with all of the information desired to complete your weekly report. A memorandum or diary of the operations connected with the construction of a road or bridge shall be kept in a book as a matter of future reference in case of disputes or for information that may be desired.

29. *Cost Records.* Keeping cost records is an essential part of your duty if you can secure authentic information. Cost record books will be furnished you for this purpose. Records should be made as

complete as possible without interfering with the supervision of th
construction work and without annoyance to the contractor or hi
timekeeper. Diplomatic methods may enable you to secure some valu
able data on specific phases of the contractor's work. In many case
contractors will cheerfully give information in regard to costs. It i
not always advisable to keep an accurate cost of all phases of the wor
but pick out a few essential operations and keep an accurate cost o
them so as to enable the Department to compile information suitable fo
making future estimates.

30. *Records of Underground Work.* You shall make a detaile
report in your permanent notebook of all substructure work in con
nection with the construction of a road or bridge. In case tile drain
are put in, the stationing and exact location of the tile, the size, deptl
etc. shall be recorded. This information, as soon as the work is com
pleted, shall be reported to the district engineer in the form of a lette
for permanent record.

31. *Record of Bridge Piling.* When piles are driven in a bridg
foundation, the depth and width of the footings, and the character o
the soil encountered shall also become a permanent record. This in
formation shall be transmitted to the district engineer in the form o
a letter setting forth the number of piles driven in each bridge, thei
size, length and spacing, the character of the soil, the depth of the foot
ings, etc. These letter records of substructure work are made so tha
they may be readily referred to in the future.

32. *Extra Work.* Field engineers are not permitted to authoriz
extra work or substantial alterations without the written consent o
the district engineer or his authorized assistant. Any changes appear
ing to be desirable shall be brought to the attention of the distric
engineer or his assistant at the earliest possible date so that the correc
tion may be made if found necessary. On all force account or extr
work you will keep a complete daily record of the number of men em
ployed and materials used. At the close of each day you will checl
your records against the official record of the contractor's foreman o
superintendent and in case of discrepancies make adjustments befor
proceeding further with the work. If it is impossible to check eacl
night for comparison, a check shall be made at least two or three time
each week to make sure that the records will agree.

Bills should be presented by the contractor upon completion of th
extra work, or at least once each month, covering all extra work auth
orized.

In no case should a contractor be expected to do extra work with
out a written order from you or the district engineer. Extra work i
often the cause of considerable dispute upon final completion of a con
tract. You should, therefore, take great pains to see that a complet
record is made of all extra work and that your records conform to th
records taken by the contractor's superintendent or foreman.

WATER SUPPLY.

33. *Quantity and Quality.* The contractor's water supply for road or bridge construction is a very vital part of the work and often affects materially the progress or quality of the construction. Ordinarily the contractor should provide 10 gallons per square yard of pavement for the operation of the mixer and the mixing of the concrete. In addition he will require from fifteen to thirty gallons of water per square yard of pavement for curing purposes. A careful investigation of the water supply therefore should be made early in the season so as to make sure that a sufficient quantity may be provided at all times to complete the work in accordance with the specifications. It is also well to make a careful examination of the quality of the water to be sure that it is not injurious to the concrete or to the steam boilers in case steam is used on the mixer.

34. *Deep Wells and Reservoirs.* In general deep wells cannot be counted upon to supply water for the average road job although in some instances they are the only source of water supply and must be used. In such cases it is desirable to construct reservoirs near the wells so that storage may be provided and surplus water impounded by 24 hours' pumping. Economical and satisfactory reservoirs may often be constructed by excavating a hole of the desired capacity. The excavated hole having side slopes of about one and one-half to one may then be trimmed until smooth and the entire surface plastered with a one to three mortar about three-fourths of an inch in thickness. The plastered surface should be protected by damp straw or canvas immediately after its application to prevent it from cracking. The reservoir may be filled with water twelve hours after it is finished.

Fig. 1. Temporary reservoir adjacent to deep well to hold surplus water during paving operations.

35. *Pipe Line.* The pipe line from the water supply to the mixing plant or road should be of sufficient size to give an ample supply

to the mixer when it is working to its full capacity. It is not always necessary that the pipe line be sufficient to supply water for curing purposes at the time the mixer is being run although this is desirable. The curing can usually be done at a time when the mixer is not in operation. The pipe line should contain a number of unions so that in case broken pipe is encountered a new section may be installed without undue delay to the work. Expansion joints at intervals of one thousand to two thousand feet are also desirable to prevent buckling or breaking of the pipe line during hot weather. Regular expansion joints are manufactured by pipe and pump companies but may be conveniently made by installing a short section of water hose at the desired intervals. The pipe line should be laid to one side of the road where it will not be distributed by grading operations. It should be so placed as to have the advantage of the shade of a hedge to protect it from the heat of the sun and also laid with T's and plugs at all low points so that it may be drained readily during freezing weather. In some cases it may be desirable to plow a furrow to receive the pipe line. The earth may then be plowed back on top of the pipe line and the water thus kept much cooler during the hot summer months and freezing prevented during the cool nights of early fall.

36. *Pipe Connections.* When the pipe line is being laid you should see that sufficient "T's" are installed at intervals of 200 to 500 feet to provide for hose connections for supplying water to the mixer and for curing purposes. Where big mixers are being operated it is frequently desirable and economical to install two independent pipe lines, one for the mixer and the other for curing purposes.

37. *Pump.* The size of pump for different jobs will vary with the amount of water needed. In general, the 30 to 40 gallon per minute pump will prove to be sufficient for the four-bag mixer. There is a great deal of discussion as to the advantages of steam vs. gas pumps. Where gas pumps are installed it is usually desirable to have duplicate units to eliminate trouble and delays. The one and one-half or two inch pipe line used with the ordinary construction pump usually limits the distance over which water may be successfully delivered to the mixer or road job. A distance of three miles is usually the maximum for a two-inch pipe line with grades ordinarily encountered. When required to pump this distance or further, it is desirable and usually necessary to install a booster pump at some convenient point in the line.

ROAD BED.

38. *Subgrade.* A uniform, well compacted, properly drained subgrade has perhaps more to do with the successful completion and life of a pavement than most any other factor. Regardless of the type of wearing surface constructed, the subgrade must necessarily transmit the loads from the pavement to the earth. The subgrade should be recognized as that portion of the road from shoulder to shoulder of the graded roadway. It should be shaped and crowned to drain the water readily to the side ditches and should be as nearly uniform in character as is possible to make it with practical methods.

In general, the subgrade that is made by the use of teams or tractors requires very little rolling to secure sufficient consolidation for the pavement. The frequent use of a road drag or planer will usually leave a subgrade in condition suitable for final finishing and placing of the pavement. Where a slight amount of material is moved in the final shaping of the subgrade, a light tandem roller will iron out the surface in a manner that prepares it satisfactorily for the pavement. Special care should be taken to get the subgrade thoroughly compacted immediately under the side forms and for a distance of at least one foot outside. The subgrade beneath the forms must support the load that is applied to the forms and prevent settlement.

39. *Scarifying and Shaping.* After the rough grading has been done, a subgrader or scarifier operated in connection with a power roller may be used to advantage. In some instances light scarifiers are used and pulled by independent power. In either case it is advisable to scarify the entire surface to a depth of at least two inches below the finished subgrade. The pulverized material may then be uniformly spread over the surface to the desired depth and the surface rolled lightly to bring it to true grade. There are a number of subgrading machines which may be used after the surface has been scarified or loosened. These machines operate on the side forms and trim the subgrade true to the cross section shown on the plans. After the subgrade has been prepared for the pavement, it should not be rutted by trucks or wagons or compacted in such a way that it will not be uniform in character.

Fig. 2. Preparing subgrade in advance of a paving mixer.

40. *Wetting Subgrade.* When trucks are employed very little water should be used for wetting the subgrade in advance of placing the concrete as water will cause some mud to get into the concrete. Under normal conditions and especially where materials are delivered by industrial quipment, the best results are obtained when the subgrade is soaked with water the day before the concrete is placed. This

method is much to be preferred and should be used whenever possible. The purpose of wetting the subgrade is to prevent the earth from absorbing an excessive amount of moisture from the concrete during the setting process and to allow the over-compacted earth in the subgrade to swell and obtain its normal condition before the pavement is laid.

41. *Rolling Subgrade.* It is necessary that some form of roller be used in the preparation of the subgrade for the pavement. Under normal conditions the light 3-ton tandem roller will prove entirely satisfactory for this purpose. However, the ordinary 3 to 5-ton horse roller pulled by a light caterpillar tractor engine will also meet the requirements of the specifications and prove to be satisfactory. In some instances the 10-ton, 3-wheeled roller will be used, in which case it should go over the subgrade but once as it is very easy to over-compact portions of the roadbed. In such case the subgrade should always be soaked 12 hours or more before concrete is placed. In general, the use of the 3-wheeled heavy type roller for this purpose should be discouraged. Where there are but a few inches of loose material to be compacted, a home-made concrete roller or a hand roller may prove to be sufficient to iron out the subgrade preparatory to the construction of the pavement. In no case should the heavy 3-wheeled rollers be used after the soil has been saturated with water as it will over-compact the earth and cause trouble in the swelling of the subgrade after the pavement is placed. The heavy rollers and traction engines are especially desirable for compacting large fills during the process of construction. The 3-wheeled, 10-ton rollers will locate the soft spots in the fill and assist in compacting the loose material and thereby reduce the settlement to a minimum. When fills are built up in horizontal layers of approximately 18 inches by the use of wheel scrapers, slips or dump wagons, there is usually no advantage in rolling the fills during the process of construction.

Fig. 3. Horse roller coupled to caterpillar tractor and used for rolling subgrade.

42. *Unrolled Subgrade.* In case the subgrade has been prepared for a distance of several hundred feet in advance of the mixer and there should be a heavy rain causing an undue swelling of the subgrade, no attempt should be made to roll in advance of the mixer or of concrete that is being deposited. In this case the use of a subgrading machine or other means of trimming the subgrade true to cross section before the concrete is deposited is sufficient. The subgrade is in an ideal condition for the pavement after a rain or after it has become thoroughly saturated by means of sprinkling as this will cause the earth to swell and assume its natural condition. The principal object in the preparation of a subgrade is to secure uniformity throughout. Should low places exist they may be filled with earth providing they are compacted the same as the remainder of the road.

43. *Driving on Subgrade.* There is no objection to motor trucks being driven over the subgrade provided they are not loaded to such an extent that the subgrade is rutted or depressed out of shape. When trucks are used for dumping directly into the mixer they should cover the entire surface of the subgrade in order to compact it more uniformly throughout its full width. Narrow steel tires or teams turning or backing on the subgrade shall not be allowed. When trucks are used for the delivery of batches direct to the mixer considerable time will be saved by utilizing a turn table which may be placed on the subgrade a few hundred feet in advance of the paving mixer. Frequent backing and turning on the subgrade often causes large ruts. This should be avoided wherever possible. There are a few truck bodies that are built so as to dump at the side thereby permitting material to be dumped directly into the skip of the mixer before the truck is turned around. This method permits the trucks to turn when empty. In this case turning on the subgrade is not nearly so objectionable.

44. *Porous Material for Subgrade.* When the subgrade is poorly drained it may often appear to be advantageous to roll in a layer of gravel, stone or cinders before placing the pavement thereon. Generally there is no objection to this method of obtaining a suitable subgrade, but in such instances the porous material beneath the pavement should be carefully drained or it will act as a reservoir for water and thereby result in additional damage to the pavement.

45. *Tiling Subgrade.* If an exceptionally wet subsoil is encountered, it may be remedied by intercepting the flow of underground water by the installation of 4 or 6-inch tile drains. Such tile should be placed from $2\frac{1}{2}$ to 3 feet in depth and the trench backfilled with porous material. A single line of tile down the center or along the upper side of the pavement with lateral drains at various intervals along the road will usually prove sufficient to drain out the surplus underground water. When two lines of tile are used, they should ordinarily be placed beneath the edges of the pavement to a depth of 2 to 3 feet and the trench backfilled with porous material. In general a 6-inch tile is a desirable size to use for the draining of the subsoil.

46. *Oiling Subgrade.* After the subgrade has been prepared it may be treated advantageously with road oil. The oil will keep down

the dust and prevent the formation of ruts and mud during rain}
weather. It will make possible the use of light trucks much soone
after a rain and will eliminate the necessity of wetting down the sub
grade prior to the placing of the concrete. For construction pur
poses the subgrade may be oiled for a width of 15 feet. This woulc
enable trucks to follow the oiled portion of the road in the delivery o
materials. If the pavement is to secure the full benefit of the oi
the subgrade should be oiled to the full width of 18 feet. The oi
should be applied as early in the spring as conditions will permit anc
when the road is free from dust and loose material. It should be ap
plied at the rate of one-half gallon per square yard in two equal appli
cations. The cost will vary but may be estimated at $300 to $600 pe
mile of road.

The subgrade that has been thoroughly saturated with oil wil
resist the raising of subsoil water by capillary attraction and will pre
vent surface water from softening the subsoil immediately beneatl
the slab, thereby resulting in additional stability to the pavement.

47. *Frozen Subgrade.* Mixed concrete should not be depositec
upon a frozen subgrade for the reason that the frost will be drawi
from the subgrade, thus lowering the temperature of the concrete be
low 40° F. and preventing it from obtaining its proper set. Whei
there is but a small amount of road to be completed during freezin}
weather the subgrade may be protected from frost by a covering o
straw, which shall be removed immediately in advance of the deposit
ing of the concrete.

48. *Materials on subgrade.* After the subgrade has been pre
pared, no materials shall be dumped upon it without the consent of th
Chief Highway Engineer. Aggregates may, however, be dumped upoi

Fig. 4. Material stored at intervals of 600 feet along the side of the
road. Short industrial track delivers material from storage piles to
paving mixer.

the subgrade or at the sides of the road at intervals of not less than 400 feet provided the material is placed in large piles and not spread out over the subgrade or shoulders. When material is dumped in this way it should be piled at least three dumps high to prevent spreading and to avoid a surplus of earth being picked up when it is rehandled.

49. *Backfilling trenches and bridge abutments.* When it is necessary to backfill a trench or the space adjacent to a bridge abutment, special effort should be made to thoroughly compact the earth. Numerous pavement failures and bridge failures are traceable directly to negligence in this important operation. The backfill must be made in *horizontal layers* of not to *exceed one foot* and each layer thoroughly compacted by means of rolling or hand tamping until the entire fill is completed. In trench work it is frequently possible to fill the trench with water and make all backfills by dumping material directly into the water; much better results will be obtained in this way, as the fill will settle very little. When back-filling bridge abutments or walls, surplus water should be pumped out before the backfill is made. If this is not done the fill will be softened to such an extent that a fluid pressure will be created that far exceeds the pressure for which the abutment or wall was designed and serious cracking or failure will be the inevitable result. Care should always be taken in backfilling around abutments and wings. All excavated space in front of wings and abutments shall be filled simultaneously with the backfill. If this is not done, failure is liable to occur. Do not permit under any conditions the puddling of back fills for abutments or the dropping of earth from a great height from drag line buckets or other excavating machinery.

LAYING PAVEMENT.

50. *Concrete Mixer.* Any type of mixer that will permit materials to be measured accurately and will mix materials to a uniform consistency in one minute of time shall be allowed. Any concrete mixer that will not turn out concrete of uniform consistency and of approximately one inch slump shall not be permitted on the work. Many mixer manufacturers will insist that their machines will mix concrete much better and in less time than competing mixers, and will want the advantage of mixing materials less than the one minute stipulated in the specifications. In no case shall preference be granted.

51. *Timing Devices.* All mixers on pavement construction shall be equipped with a mechanical timing device which shall warn the mixer operator when all materials in the drum have been mixed for one full minute. If the timing device is out of order a reasonable time should be allowed the contractor for securing repairs but in no case shall he be allowed more than 72 hours unless he shows sufficient reason to justify further consideration such as delay in the delivery of the repair parts.

All materials, including the water, for each batch of concrete shall be mixed at least one minute while the drum of the mixer revolves at the speed for which it was designed. In a few instances contractor will persist in discharging the mixer 5 to 10 seconds in advance of th one minute time specified. This practice will not be tolerated.

52. *Charging Mixer.* Inasmuch as the specifications will not per mit material to be dumped on the subgrade, paving mixers must neces sarily be charged by means of batch boxes delivered to the side of th mixer by industrial railway cars, trucks, or wagons, or by means o dump wagons or motor driven vehicles which may be arranged to dum materials directly into the skip of the mixer.

53. *Installation of Corrugated Joints.* Corrugated metal joint shall be staked securely in place with heavy (No. 9) wire which ma be left in the concrete, or by means of small iron stakes that may b removed after the concrete has been deposited and partially shape to the cross section desired. Frequent inspection of corrugated joint shall be made during the finishing operations to make sure they hav not been displaced. Where conditions will permit, the central joint ma be staked into place in advance of the paving mixer.

The corrugated metal strips will usually be purchased in 10-foc lengths. They may be staked in place with the ends lapped at the joint with butt joints, or with open joints so that the transverse reinforcin bars may be inserted through the openings. The transverse bars ma be put in at the joints or at intermediate points by means of punchin the corrugated metal or slotting it to one-half its depth.

54. *Tie Bars.* The deformed, transverse dowell or tie bar should be anchored into place before the concrete is deposited or the may be worked into place after the concrete in the pavement has bee partially shaped. The longitudinal bars may be held in place by iro stakes or chairs, or they may be laid on the subgrade and worked u into place after the concrete has been deposited. In the latter cas extreme care should be taken to see that the concrete thoroughly su rounds the bars and that they are properly located when the pavemei is finished.

55. *Subgrade Templates.* A template cut to the true crown (the subgrade shall be kept in advance of the spreading of the coi crete to insure that the subgrade conforms to the desired cross se(tion. When a paving mixer is used the template may be kept betwee the mixer and concrete, or, it may be kept ahead of the placing of th longitudinal steel and central corrugated metal joint. When truck are used for delivering batch boxes or mixed concrete, the templai shall be set in place frequently to insure that the subgrade has th proper cross section before the concrete is deposited and finished.

The template shall be made from sound wood and of sufficiei length to rest upon the side forms. It shall be cut so that spikes drive about 6 inches apart may project about 2 inches from the lower edg of the timber and so that the heads of the spikes will conform to th true cross section of the subgrade when the template is resting on th side forms. The template shall be moved longitudinally on the sic forms and if the nail heads mar the subgrade, sufficient earth shall l removed so that the heads will just touch the subgrade. If the ten pate is used after the longitudinal corrugated joints and steel have been placed, it shall be notched so that it will not interfere with the metal or steel bars. If a mechanical subgrader is used, the template will not have to be used as frequently as when the subgrade is made by hand. A template should always be on the job, however, and used frequently to insure getting the full thickness of pavement specified. Keep in mind that the finished pavement shall always be not less than the cross section specified. A greater thickness is not objectionable but is not wanted.

56. *Header Boards.* When header boards are installed at the noon day hour or at the completion of a day's work, the longitudinal bars shall pass through a slot in the header board a distance of at least 2 feet to provide for the proper lapping of the bars at the joints. The central longitudinal metal joint shall butt against the corrugated header board.

Header boards preferably should be made of one-fourth inch metal corrugated the same as standard corrugated metal. If this type of header is too expensive, a 2 or 3-inch timber carefully cut to the crown of the road and faced with heavy corrugated metal screwed or tacked into place may be used. There is no object in leaving the corrugated metal in place at construction joints so it may be fastened directly to the wood header. Extreme care should be exercised in setting header boards at the noon hour and upon completion of the day's work. They should be set so that they will not be higher than the remainder of the pavement. Before the concrete is finally finished at the header board, it shall be checked with a 10-foot straight edge to make sure that it conforms to the true cross section and grade of the surface of the pavement.

57. *Noon Day Construction Joints.* During the hot summer months when there is more than one-half hour's delay in placing concrete, a header board shall be set the same as when the work is completed at the close of the day. If this is not done, the concrete in the tapered joint will paritally set and an imperfect bond will be formed. The tapered joint will make a weak plane in the concrete which will likely be the cause for a "blow-up" when the pavement is subjected to excessive temperature stresses. The object of the corrugated metal or surface is to obtain a dovetailing effect between the two slabs thereby preventing displacement and further aiding in distributing concentrated loads that may be applied adjacent to the construction joints.

58. *Construction Joints.* Construction joints should be installed at the close of each day's work and during the hot summer months at the close of work at noon provided the noon period is thirty minutes or more. All construction joints shall have a corrugated surface. This can be secured either by laying corrugated metal adjacent to the header board or by securely fastening corrugated metal to the header board. The corrugated metal may be removed when work is resumed. All construction joints should be carefully checked with a 10-foot straight edge immediately after the concrete has been

shaped to make sure that they do not vary more than one-fourth inch from the true alignment of the surface of the road. As soon as the concrete has taken its initial set the construction joints as well as the edge of the pavement shall be neatly edged with an edging tool having a one-half inch radius. There is no excuse for construction joints being built high or low. Any joint that deviates more than one-fourth inch from a 10-foot straight edge will be rejected and the best time to correct the defect is before the concrete takes its initial set.

59. *Late Fall Construction.* Late fall construction should always be protected by an ample covering of earth or straw for a period of at least five days after the concrete has been finished to protect it from a sudden drop in temperature. In nearly every instance the contractor who attempts to finish a pavement in November will have a portion of his work injured by freezing. Extreme care should therefore be taken to see that the road is amply covered so that the proper quality of concrete may be secured and the contractor saved from unnecessary expense. If the contractor attempts to do much late fall construction he should provide plenty of canvas or felt covered frames preferably the kind that arch over the pavement leaving a space of at least two feet between the surface of the pavement and the canvas or felt. Oil burners or salamanders may then be installed beneath the covering to generate sufficient heat to enable the pavement to harden so that the road may be covered with earth or straw without marring the surface. When concrete work is carried on during very cold or freezing weather it is desirable to heat the water before it goes into the mixture, or to use some other method that will raise the temperature of the mix to above 40° F. before it is deposited and finished in the road. Water may be conveniently heated by raising the pipe line adjacent to the mixer for a distance of 50 to 100 feet and building a fire beneath it. The materials in the drum may be heated by special oil burning devices that are now on the market. They may be operated inside of the mixer drum and used to raise the temperature of the mix several degrees during the period of mixing. Concrete can not be successfully finished if its temperature is below 40° F., hence a special effort should be made to have the material at a temperature of 40° or higher for a period of at least five days after it is deposited.

60. *One-half of Pavement Built at a Time.* Where the standard 18-foot section is used having a central longitudinal corrugated joint, the pavement may be built one-half at a time. If this method is followed a 9-foot section may be built and finished with the finishing machine the same as a standard 18-foot pavement, there being however, no longitudinal reinforcing bar in the pavement adjacent to the center line. The transverse bars should pass through the forms at the center points or at the joints, and after the forms are removed the bars may be bent to one side at an angle of 90° provided they are bent to a radius of at least four inches. When the second half of the pavement is built the bars shall be bent back into place. Extreme care should be taken to see that the bars are clean and that the bending

does not break the old concrete. Where the road is built in halves, the contractor may remove the central corrugated metal strip if he so desires. There is no object in the metal remaining in place as the corrugated surface in the concrete and the transverse reinforcing bars form the interlocking joint which is needed for transferring loads from one side of the joint to the other. The last half of the pavement should be finished with a specially designed finishing machine that will operate on the finished pavement and one side form. When the pavement is constructed in two 9-foot strips, the central joint shall be edged with an edging tool having a radius of one-half inch.

61. *Side Forms for Pavements.* Pressed steel forms shall be used for all pavement construction. They shall be set true to line and grade and staked in such a manner that they will not deviate more than one-fourth inch from a 10-foot straight edge after the material has been deposited and finished. It will be necessary, therefore, that extreme care be used in securing a uniform, well compacted subgrade, immediately beneath the side forms. If the earth will not support the side forms, stakes may be driven beneath the forms at frequent intervals to strengthen the supporting power of the earth. All steel forms shall be oiled after each day's use. The standard 10-foot steel forms should be used for all curves having a radius of 200 feet or more. If the radius is less than 200 feet, better results will ordinarily be obtained by using 2 x 8 wood forms around the curve, as the wood may be sprung and staked and made to conform more nearly to the curve desired. Where wood forms are used, they should be oiled to prevent the concrete from adhering to them. When the alignment of a 10-foot steel section deviates more than one-fourth inch from a 10-foot straight edge, it should be rejected and not used in the work until it is straightened. Bent or battered forms shall be rejected. Resident engineers and inspectors should frequently check with the eye the vertical and horizontal alignment of the side forms, both before and after the concrete has been deposited. Kinks and unnecessary waves and all irregularities shall be immediately corrected.

62. *Proportioning Aggregates and Cement.* Contractors shall provide a means on the job for proportioning aggregates. Two boxes, one holding one cubic foot and one holding 0.95 of a cubic foot shall be provided for measuring mixed concrete and aggregates. Cement, unless delivered in bulk, shall be measured in sacks. The theorectical amount of cement needed for a given section of road shall be determined by mixing with water, until the desired consistency is secured, one bag of cement with the fine and coarse aggregates in the proportions specified for the class of work being done. The mixed concrete shall then be tamped in the one cubic foot box and thus measured to determine definitely the exact number of cubic feet of mixed concrete that may be obtained from one bag of cement: e. g., the cement for Class X concrete (proportions 1:2:3½) shall be determined by mixing one bag of cement with two accurately measured boxes of sand and 3½ boxes of coarse aggregate with sufficient water to secure the desired consistency. The box used for proportioning

aggregates as specified in the preceding sentence shall have a capacity of 0.95 of a cubic foot. The mixed concrete shall then be tamped and measured in a box having a capacity of one cubic foot. Several such tests shall be made so as to eliminate slight variations in aggregates. Whenever there is a radical change in the characteristics of aggregates a new series of tests shall be made to determine the theoretical amount of cement required.

This method will enable you to determine definitely the amount of cement in bags needed for one cubic yard of concrete or 100 feet of pavement using the materials available. After the concreting is begun and occasionally as the work progresses, the material for one batch shall be carefully measured (using the 0.95 cubic foot box) so that you, as well as the men handling the materials, may become familiar with the proper proportions. When the work is first begun all batches shall be very carefully measured and the subgrade carefully shaped so that you can check the exact number of sacks of cement required for each 25 or 100 feet of road. If the pavement is built exactly according to cross section and the proportions accurately measured, you should check closely the amount of cement required as determined by the use of the one cubic foot box. At the end of each 100 feet, and at the end of a day's run, the sacks shall be counted and a record made of the amount of cement used in each 100 feet of pavement and the total used during the day. All of this information shall be shown in your memorandum record book together with the exact station numbers.

The following table of quantities for a 16 and 18 foot concrete pavement will aid in determining the materials needed for a given section of road.

MATERIALS NEEDED FOR A 16-FOOT PAVEMENT HAVING A UNIFORM THICKNESS OF 7 INCHES.

	Cement bbls.	Fine agg. cu. yds.	Coarse agg. cu. yds.	Concrete cu. yds.	Corrugated iron lbs.	¾" o smooth bar, lbs.	¾" deformed bar, lbs.
100 feet..	55.65	16.64	29.22	34.57	60.00	333.33	52.00
1 mile....	2,938.32	878.59	1,542.82	1,825.30	3,168.00	17,599.82	2,745.60
1 sq. yd..	.313	.094	.164	.194	.338	1.875	.293

MATERIALS NEEDED FOR AN 18-FOOT PAVEMENT HAVING A UNIFORM THICKNESS OF 7 INCHES,

	Cement bbls.	Fine agg. cu. yds.	Coarse agg. cu. yds.	Concrete cu. yds.	Corrugated iron lbs.	¾" o smooth bar, lbs.	¾" deformed bar, lbs.
100 feet..	62.61	18.72	32.87	38.88	60.00	333.33	52.00
1 mile....	3,305.81	988.42	1,735.54	2,052.86	3,168.00	17,599.82	2,745.60
1 sq. yd..	.313	.094	.164	.194	.300	1.667	.260

Note.—Assumptions:—1 bbl. of cement = 3.8 cu. ft. Voids = 45%. Excess of agg. = 7%. Length of ¾" o bars 20'. 1 cu. yd. requires 1.61 bbls. cement— 0.45 cu. yds. Sand—0.79 cu. yds. Stone for 1-2-3½ mixture.

63. *Combination Truck and Industrial Railroad Delivery.* Batch boxes may be delivered to a paving mixer by means of industrial

cars on tracks at the side of the road very economically. This method permits the subgrade to remain in perfect condition until the concrete has been placed. In a few instances a combination of truck and industrial delivery of material has been used to advantage. Where

Fig. 5. One and one-half ton pneumatic tired truck delivering mixed concrete from central plant to road.

Fig. 6. Aggregate stored on top of a tunnel permits large storage of material and easy method of filling batch boxes on industrial railroad equipment.

the road to be improved extends from the material yard it is often possible to build the first one or two miles by the use of a short industrial track. The subsequent mileage can be built by trucking the material over the improved road which is at least 30 days old, then transferring the batch boxes to industrial cars that operate on the shoulder. This method of hauling takes advantage of industrial delivery to the mixer and truck haul on the improved road that has obtained its full strength. The transfer of batch boxes from trucks to industrial cars can usually be made at a very nominal expense.

Fig. 7. Concrete pavement cured by ponding method. Note tunnel and material yard and cement storage bins in background.

Fig. 8. Material plant for central proportioning batch boxes for industrial railroad delivery.

64. *Team Delivery to Mixer.* On roads that have sufficient right-of-way to provide a reasonably good earth road on either side of the pavement, batch boxes of material may be delivered direct

to the mixer by team haul. A derrick on the mixer, or independent
of the mixer, may be used to lift the batch boxes from the wagons
and discharge them into the skip of the mixer. This method frequently requires a temporary bridge over the pavement so that the
teams may cross the newly laid pavement and return on the opposite
side of the road. Team delivery usually proves economical on short
hauls.

Fig. 9. Transfer station for material boxes from trucks to industrial
cars. Industrial cars deliver materials to paving mixer about one mile
ahead.

65. *Proportioning Materials in Batch Boxes.* When Batch Boxes
are used to deliver material to the mixer, the sand and coarse aggregate should be measured preferably by means of separate compart-
ments in the batch box. However, the sand and coarse aggregate
may be dumped into the same compartment provided care is taken
to see that each batch box is filled to the required height with aggregate, or filled from hoppers that will measure accurately the materials. It is desirable that batch boxes contain a separate compartment for cement although this is not necessary if the batches are
used within a few hours after they are filled and are not exposed to
rain. Where the aggregate and cement are dumped into one compartment at the material yard, a plant inspector to check all batches
shall be provided in addition to the inspector out on the road where
the pavement is being built. If the cement is delivered to the paving
mixer by placing a given number of sacks on top of each batch box,
and the sacks emptied when the batch reaches the paving mixer, ordinarily no plant inspector is required. In this instance the inspector
at the paving mixer should examine carefully the batch boxes when
delivered to make sure that all have been filled with aggregate to
the proper height and that the proper number of sacks is on each
batch. Cement delivered in sacks on top of the batch boxes can
usually be saved in case of a wreck on the delivery system. It will

also insure the proper amount for each batch as well as protect from wind and from moisture in the aggregate.

CEMENT.

66. *Protecting Cement in Transit to Mixer.* If the cement dumped on top of the aggregate in the batch boxes at the material ya some method of covering each batch shall be provided so as to prote it from rain and wind while in transit. There is no objection to allo' ing cement to come in contact with the wet aggregate for about o hour. There is, however, serious objection to allowing it to lie (top or between the sand and coarse aggregate more than an hour, the cement will frequently cake and lose a portion of its value.

67. *Bulk Cement.* Bulk cement may be used provided suitab devices are installed at the storage plant to accurately weigh or measu the amount of cement in each batch of material. A means of weighin the required amount of cement is preferable to a measuring metho although measuring will be satisfactory if a device is provided that w cause the material to be disturbed uniformly as it enters the measurin hopper so that the same amount in bulk will be provided in each batc The measuring hopper shall also be open when it is filled so that ea batch may be carefully examined to see that it contains the requir amount of cement. Bulk cement may be shipped in open top gondo cars and unloaded by means of a clam shell, but in such cases ea car shall be provided with a suitable canvas covering to protect it fro the weather during transit. Each car in this case shall be examin upon delivery to ascertain the amount of cement damaged or ceme lost in transit. Any cement lost in this manner will be charged the contractor and he will have to make proper adjustments with tl cement company or shipper. Railroad weights on bulk delivery of c ment are always subject to considerable error. Accurate record, ther fore, shall be kept of all batches used of the bulk cement and th record used as a check on the total bulk cement delivered. When bu cement is delivered in box cars it may be unloaded by means of shove ing, drag lines or air suction. In any case, care shall be used to se that no surplus material is wasted by being blown away.

68. *Cement in Sacks.* When the State purchases cement tl sacks are charged to the contractor. The contractor is therefore r sponsible for the care of the sacks and for the credit which he receiv on them when they are returned to the cement companies. Cemer companies usually tack a card on the inside of the car showing tl amount of cement contained in the car according to the mill coun In case the contents check short of the amount shown on the card (bill of lading, this card shall be sent in with your complete report t the district engineer.

Immediately upon receipt of a car of cement the car number, in itials, and seal number shall be obtained. The seal number is very in portant, as in case of damage or shortage it is necessary to show tha the original seal number was on the car when it was delivered. As soo

is the seal is broken the cement becomes the property of the contractor
and he is then held responsible for its care and use. Before any cement is removed from the car all cement sacks shall be counted if the
material is piled in such a way as to permit this; otherwise a careful
check shall be made on the number of sacks in the car as the material
is unloaded.

69. *Damaged Cement.* If there is any damaged cement a very
careful record shall be made of the number of sacks and a description
made of the cause of damage. When there is any great amount of
defective material in the car it is well to get into communication with
the railroad agent and bring the matter to his attention and get his no-
tation on the freight bill. A careful check should also be made of the
damaged sacks that are unusable at the time the cement is unloaded.
If there is a large number of damaged sacks, the bill with the nota-
tion thereon shall be forwarded promptly to the district engineer with
a complete explanation of the shortage or the damaged material so
that he may file claim with the cement company without delay. In
all cases the unusable sacks shall be found in separate bundles when
returned to the cement company so that proper credit can be given to
the contractor.

70. *Cement Records and Reports.* Practically all of the above
information should be obtained by a representative of the contractor.
However, if you have a material yard inspector he should secure all
of this information first hand. If there is but one inspector on the job
and you do not have time to check any of the materials as they are
received at destination you should make a special effort to secure
all the information from the contractor at the close of each day. Cement shall be reported to the district office on regular cards. These
cards shall be made only from actual knowledge of the receipt of the
cars and any discrepancies in the amount of cement in the car from the
amount shown on the testing engineer's card shall be noted on the
report. A very careful record of cement shipments shall be kept and
the resident engineer shall keep himself informed as to the actual dis-
position of every car of cement reported to his job.

71. *Cleaning Cement Sacks.* When the cement sacks are emptied
into batch boxes or mixers, caution the men emptying the sacks to shake
each one thoroughly. Laborers often become very careless in the hand-
ing of cement sacks and frequently leave one or two pounds of cement
in each sack. This, in some cases, may be intentional as the contractor
will clean the sacks with a cleaning machine and thereby obtain considerable additional cement. With the ordinary cleaning machine it
is possible to save enough cement even after a thorough shaking of
the sacks to pay for the machine in one or two season's work. Thorough cleaning of the sacks by means of machines should be encouraged
as it will enable the contractor to obtain some additional cement and
reduce the cost of return freight on empty sacks.

72. *Storing Cement.* Contractors should arrange to store a portion of their cement on all work which they have to do. It is practically
impossible to depend upon regular cement shipments due to delays at

the cement plant and to railroad transportation. In general, a cor tractor should store approximately 25 per cent of his requirements t prevent delays. Cement ordinarily can be most economically stored i especially built warehouses, adjacent to the railroad siding. Thes warehouses may be built by placing cross stringers or sleepers directl upon the earth or upon cinders and laying two-inch planking longitud inally. The flooring should be covered with tar paper or a good thick ness of dry straw to prevent circulation of air. The floor should b independent of the side walls so that irregular settlement will not wrec the warehouse. Cement buildings are usually 14 to 16 feet in width, 1 to 16 feet in height and from 80 to 100 feet in length.

In storing cement the sacks should be packed as closely togethe as possible leaving a space of about one foot between the sacks an the side walls. If the cement is to remain in storage throughout th winter it is advisable to pack the space between the cement and sid walls with dry straw. Cement should be covered with tar paper, canva or straw so as to prevent circulation of air. If the sacks are stacke carefully you can allow about 1.1 cubic feet for each sack. When stor age cement is being used it shall be examined very carefully. In ever case frequent samples shall be taken and tested before it is used in th work. If it contains lumps they shall be screened out before the cemer is used.

73. *Cement Tests.* For each car of cement received on the jo you should receive a card from the testing engineer showing the cor tents of the car and whether or not it is acceptable. In case you re ceive a car of rejected cement, report it immediately to the testin engineer and await instructions for the disposal of the car. If the cor tractor is authorized to secure a small amount of cement locally, should be tested and you shall select a small sample in accordance wit established practice and forward to the testing engineer at the Spring field office that a record may be kept of its quality.

74. *Borrowing or Buying Cement.* If, for reasons beyond th control of the contractor, cement does not arrive when it is needed an he has ordered it a reasonable time in advance, he may be authorize to borrow or purchase some cement locally. Should this situation arise communicate with your district engineer at once so that he may issu proper authorizations.

MATERIALS.

75. *Material Tests.* All aggregates will generally be tested at th shipping point and you should receive a card from the testing enginee showing that the material is acceptable. In case you should receive car of material which it is evident does not comply with the specifica tions, you shall delay using it until you have submitted a sample to th testing engineer and have received his report. In a few instances ma terial received may be entirely satisfactory but may become mixed wit dirt or other foreign material on the job so that it is not fit for us in concrete construction. Such material should be rejected by you o

at least reported to the district engineer and his decision secured before the material is used in the work.

76. *Storing Material.* Contractors are compelled to store considerable aggregate to insure constant and uniform operation of the plant. When the material is unloaded by clam shells it is frequently stored in large piles. The clam shell operator will ordinarily dump the material in the center of the storage pile. This will soon result in a very large percentage of the coarse material rolling down the sides leaving a core that contains an excess of fine material. When the aggregate is rehandled for use it will not be properly graded and the best results cannot be secured. The separation of the materials may be very largely avoided by building up the storage pile in horizontal layers instead of dumping all the material at the one central point.

CENTRAL MIXING PLANTS.

77. Many advantages are claimed for central mixing plants. The chief advantage is perhaps the centralization of operations which permits more careful and intense supervision. Also, the ordinary stationary mixer may be used which will permit a large volume of concrete to be turned out at less expense than with a standard paver. It is frequently much easier to obtain a satisfactory supply of water for a central plant than for a field mixer. The single pipe line on the road is not overburdened by supplying water for use in the paver in addition to the use for curing purposes. The central mixers frequently are of such size that the materials may actually be mixed more than one minute and still supply all the concrete that it is possible to haul and finish during the day. There is some advantage in the extra time of mixing, as it will insure a better quality of concrete and a more workable mix both of which are an advantage to the contractor. A central plant also gives the contractor an opportunity to work out many labor saving devices thereby enabling him to mix concrete at a minimum cost.

78. *Hauling Mixed Concrete.* On many sections of road work concrete may be mixed at a central plant and then delivered to the road by means of trucks. Specifications allow a period of 40 minutes from the time the concrete is mixed until it is deposited in the road. This time is stipulated to prevent a partial set of the concrete before it is deposited in the work. Experience has shown that where a contractor attempts to haul material a distance which requires more than 40 minutes of time he is not doing his work economically. During the hot summer months 40 minutes is usually longer than the contractor should count on to haul mixed concrete. Early in the spring or late in the fall there would be no objection to holding the concrete twice the time stipulated. In general, the engineer should not concern himself with the time that mixed concrete has been held, but should see that the concrete when delivered to the road is properly spread and finished in the pavement. When mixed concrete cannot be satisfactorily finished it has undoubtedly been held in transit too long and should be rejected.

Mixed concrete will ordinarily be delivered in one to two-ton trucks having pneumatic tires. The pneumatic tires facilitate speed and prevent serious injury to the subgrade, and are therefore more desirable for hauling mixed concrete.

Fig. 10. One-ton truck loaded with mixed concrete being turned on subgrade.

Fig. 11. Central Mixing Plant.

79. *Consistency of Mixed Concrete.* When mixed concrete is to be hauled any distance extreme care should be taken to see that the consistency of the concrete is uniformly stiff. The aggregate in sloppy concrete will segregate while in transit and will be not only unsatisfactory for use in pavements but extremely difficult to dump from an ordinary truck body. After the mixed concrete is delivered

at destination the truck load should have but a small film of water on the surface and when the material is dumped should show a uniform consistency and mix. Mixed concrete has been hauled for a distance of five or six miles over ordinary country roads even in the hottest weather without injury to the concrete.

80. *Finishing Mixed Concrete.* Experience has shown that it requires additional labor to shape and finish mixed concrete that has been hauled for some distance. In no case should retempering of the delivered concrete be permitted. If extra labor cannot finish the concrete as it should be, it shall be thrown out and fresh material put in its place.

FINISHING CONCRETE PAVEMENTS.

81. *Finishing Machine.* Some form of mechanical tamper and finisher is required to finish concrete roads in accordance with specifications. It is necessary, therefore, to examine very carefully the finishing machine that is being used to see that the templets are cut to the desired crown so that the finished pavement will have the required cross section. It is also necessary to watch the machine frequently to see that it is in proper adjustment so that both sides of the road are completed alike. Frequently the tension on one side of the finishing machine is weakened resulting in a very small vertical motion and non-uniform results. The finishing belt shall be cleaned at the close of each day's work and kept soft by means of soaking in water or oil so that it is pliable at all times. The drip pan beneath the engine shall be tight to prevent oil from dripping on the newly laid concrete. Machine oil on green concrete usually causes serious disintegration. The purpose of a finishing machine is to strike off the slight amount of extra concrete that is deposited in the road and to thoroughly tamp and finish it to the desired crown. In most instances the workmen who spread the concrete do not get it to the true crown, often leaving high spots for the finishing machine to pull down, or in other words, leave a large percentage of their work to be done by the finishing machine. Where the machine is required to push ahead a large surplus of concrete it is sure to be injured, and further will leave an uneven surface in the finished pavement. The machine should normally push two or three inches of concrete ahead of the strike-off templet to insure uniform results. If the machine is required to push more than this amount of concrete it will naturally drag more of the concrete ahead than it should and for this reason leave low spots or depressions in the finished pavement. If the proper amount of concrete is deposited between the forms the machine will usually finish the pavement true to the top of the forms and will not push any surplus concrete over the side. If the templets are properly adjusted they will usually clean the forms thereby insuring a much more uniform and even surface.

82. *Checking Finished Surface.* After the machine has passe
over the forms two or three times the finished grade of the form
should be checked either with the eye or by the use of a 10-foc
straight edge. If they deviate more than one-fourth inch from th
10-foot straight edge they have probably been driven into the groun
by overtamping or by not having been properly supported. If settle
ment has occurred, the forms should immediately be adjusted t
grade and additional material spread upon the surface of the road be
fore the final finishing and belting. This is absolutely necessary t
insure the proper finish to the pavement.

Fig. 12. Porous spots in concrete surface can be avoided if a small
amount of concrete is kept in advance of the templet when the finishing
machine is moved forward.

83. *Overtamping Surface.* Ordinarily concrete that is deposite
on the road can be finished by passing the machine over the surfac
four or five times. In many instances concrete roads are overtampec
If this is done a surplus of laitance is brought to the surface of th
road and the side forms are settled and usually an unsatisfactor
alignment and surface finish are the result. When convenient, accurat
measurements should be taken at given points on the finished sub
grade and similar measurements taken after the pavement has bee
finished to see just what thickness of concrete has actually been se
cured. Frequently finishing machines settle the side forms as muc
as one-half inch and you will get a corresponding reduction in th
finished thickness of the pavement.

84. *Final Finish.* The final belting of a pavement can be don
with a hand belt or with the belt on the finishing machine. Eithe
will give a desirable finish, if used just prior to the initial set of th
concrete. The final belting shall ordinarily be done from 50 to 10
feet behind the mixer. When 500 to 800 feet of concrete is being lai
per day it is necessary to follow the finishing machine with a belt oper
ated by hand as the ordinary finishing machine is not designed to tam

and finish a greater volume of work. If more than 800 lineal feet is laid per day it is necessary to have at least two finishing machines on the job.

85. *Hand Roller and Belt.* A belt that can be operated by hand as well as a small hand roller and a hand tamping templet shall be on each job at all times so that they can be put into operation immediately upon a break down of the finishing machine. If this is not done and a break down occurs it may often be necessary to remove the concrete —an operation which would entail considerable expense.

86. *Finishing Curves.* The hand tamping templet, roller and belt are necessary for finishing around curves having a radius of less than 200 feet. On the maximum superelevated curves the finishing machine causes considerable trouble by forcing the soft concrete to the lower side of the pavement thereby giving an irregular or poor finish in the surface of the pavement. The free use of a hand tamper, roller and belt will insure a much better surface on the superelevated curves.

Fig. 13. Ten-foot straight edge shows up a depression of three-fourths inch in the finished surface.

87. *Use of 10-foot Straight Edge.* As soon as the concrete road has been finished it shall be carefully checked for high and low spots. The 10-foot straight edge will enable you to find these spots. The concrete surface shall be carefully checked with the eye as well as with the straight edge before it takes its initial set so that the surface may be corrected by removing or adding material. If a given spot is found to be low or high it shall be immediately marked by scratching the surface after which it should be called to the attention of the superintendent or foreman in charge. Do not wait until the next day when the concrete has taken its final set as then it will be very difficult to correct the surface. In case a high or low spot was overlooked during the day's work it shall be immediately checked the following

morning before the road is covered with earth or curing material. If the surface deviates at any one place more than one-fourth inch from the 10-foot straight edge it shall be immediately trimmed off and fresh mortar floated into the surface so as to give the pavement the desired cross section and finish. There is no excuse for a pavement being built with a deviation in its surface of more than one-fourth inch from a 10-foot straight edge. Pavements having a greater deviation will not be accepted; hence the surface should be corrected before the concrete takes its initial set.

Fig. 14. Slope-wall construction to protect road from excessive erosion.

88. *Character of Finished Pavement.* The efficiency of the engineer in charge as well as that of the contractor is generally judged by the riding qualities of the finished pavement. A road may be 100 per cent perfect in all of its other qualifications but if it has a poor finish the work is condemned by the traveling public and the engineer and contractor subjected to severe criticism. On the other hand, the qualities of a pavement may not be up to standard yet if it has a perfect finish the work will have the appearance of having been carefully done and it will at least give some satisfaction to the traveling public. An uneven surface is not only unsatisfactory to the public but is frequently the cause of the destruction of the pavement. Tests have shown that a one-fourth inch deviation in the surface will impose impact loads of from two to five times the weight of the load.

SPECIAL SECTIONS.

89. *Curb and Gutter Sections.* Curb and gutter sections should be used on practically all grades that are 4 per cent or more, on heavy cut sections to save excavation, and on long slopes where the side ditches or shoulders are subjected to erosion. The chief pur-

poses of the curb and gutter sections are to carry the water in the gutter or upon the road to the bottom of the grade where it may be discharged without washing the road, and to prevent the side slopes from sloughing off and filling the ditches. Where the curb and gutter is carried to the culvert a very careful plan shall be worked out to dispose of the water. Curb sections may be built monolithic with the pavement or separate from the pavement at the desire of the contractor. In general, the contractor will choose to build the pavement first so that he may use his standard finishing machine. If this is done, the tie' rods should be inserted in the pavement at the intervals specified and a longitudinal bar placed in the curb and gutter section to give it the desired supporting strength. If proper forms are made for the curb and gutter it can be built very rapidly and will conform to the cross section details shown on the plans. Considerable hand work will have to be done to get the desired finish. There is no reason why it should not be finished just as smoothly as the remainder of the road. Special care should be taken to see that the face and back of the curbs are in perfect alignment so that the road will present the desired appearance. The back of the curb line should be edged with a one-fourth to one-half inch edging tool.

90. *Curb and Gutter Turnouts.* At the bottom of steep slopes where curb and gutter sections are used the turnout for the water will ordinarily be constructed at the junction of the cut and fill sections. However, if the fill is on a steep grade it would be advisable to continue the curb or gutter section to the culvert or to some point where the grade has flattened to such an extent that the surface water may

Fig. 15. Curb and gutter outlet at bottom of steep grade.

be readily conducted down the side of the embankment. If the take-off gutter is built too far up on the hill slope the surface water will accumulate adjacent to the pavement on the filled section and continue to cause excessive maintenance. Where it is possible to continue the curb or gutter to the culvert the water may be discharged through the head wall if an apron is provided in the bed of the stream just beneath the opening to prevent scouring. In a few instances it may be taken through the top of the culvert box, although in general, this should be discouraged as it is necessary to have the water pass through the reinforcing bars or some other grating which will eventually become clogged and cause serious damage on account of overflow.

Fig. 16. Gutter section on steep grade and through a heavy cut.

Fig. 17. Curb and gutter construction on steep grades and through heavy cuts.

91. *Grate Bars.* The installation of sewer pipe and grate bars in a curb or gutter line should be discouraged as invariably foreign material will collect over the grate and the sewer will fail to function at a time when it is most needed.

4

5

92. *Gutter Section.* When a semi-circular shaped gutter is built adjacent to the edge of the slab the earth shall be carefully shaped to the desired cross section. A form board shall then be set for the outside edge of the gutter section and the concrete poured and molded to the desired shape before it takes its initial set. In any case where a curb or semi-circular gutter is used to conduct water it shall be turned very gradually away from the road at the bottom of the hill. Any abrupt turn in the gutter will cause the water to overflow and this will result in serious erosion on the shoulder beyond the point where the gutter turns off.

CURING.

93. Newly laid concrete pavements shall be kept moist for a period of at least two weeks. Brick pavements with a cement grout filler shall be kept moist for at least 10 days.

94. *Ponding Method of Curing.* The surest, and possibly the most desirable method that may be used for curing pavements, is to pond the water on the surface of the road. This can be done by building dykes along the edges of the pavement and cross dykes at intervals of from 5 to 50 feet to prevent water from flowing down the grades.

95. *Use of Straw for Curing.* Some soil will not hold water, hence it is impossible to use the ponding method for curing. In such cases it is desirable to use six or eight inches of half rotten straw.

Fig. 18. Canvas covering on newly laid concrete pavement to protect it from sun and wind. Canvas should be kept wet when weather is extremely hot.

The partially decayed straw, with as much chaff in it as it is possible to secure, will lie close to the pavement and hold moisture for a considerable time. The straw covering can be very easily advanced as soon as the surface has been cured the desired time. If straw can be secured at a reasonable price this method of curing will probably prov as desirable and economical as any method that could be followed.

96. *Earth Covering.* A common method which is used for cu ing is that of covering the pavement with at least two inches of loo earth which may be shoveled from the sides of the road and th material kept moist by frequent sprinkling. The earth preferabl should be plowed before it is shoveled on to the pavement. In man cases the contractor can have this covering done on the unit pri basis thereby securing more desirable and economical results. Th earth covering shall be sprinkled frequently to keep the pavement moi: for the required time. In all cases the edges of the pavement shall l banked and cured the same as the surface.

Fig. 19. Canvas covered frames used to cover a concrete road immediately behind the paving mixer.

97. *Protecting Pavement by Use of Frames and Canvas.* I every case concrete pavements shall be covered by 10 o'clock A. M on the day after the work has been finished. During the hot summe months it is necessary to cover the pavement and keep it moist ju: as closely behind the mixer as it is possible to work without marrin the surface of the road. Pavement that is laid during these months sha be protected by the use of frames covered with canvas or other ma terial that will keep the sun and wind from the surface of the roadway Usually 100 feet of such frames is sufficient to protect the soft cor crete that has been finished and to prevent it from hair checking o drying out too rapidly. Following the frames the canvas may be lai directly upon the surface. In no case, however, should canvas be lai on the surface of soft concrete as it will mar the finish and make very undesirable. In some instances the contractor may arrange fo the frames to be fastened to wheels that run on the side forms. Wher this is done the frames may be pulled ahead as the finishing machin completes its work. The pavement can be covered with straw o earth after the curing frames have been moved forward.

98. *Experimental Methods of Curing Pavements.* There are other methods that are being used to some extent in the curing of pavements, although they have not as yet been perfected and should not be used unless specific instructions have been received from the Chief Highway Engineer. They may be listed as follows:

1. An oil covering of 60 to 90 per cent asphaltum content applied hot at the rate of one-third gallon per square yard. The purpose of the oil is to prevent evaporation of the moisture that is in the concrete. Tests indicate that concrete will obtain its full strength if all water used in the original mix is retained.

2. A blanket of one-eighth to three-sixteenths of an inch thick of a heavy grade of asphalt such as might be used for ordinary brick filler (35 to 60 penetration) may be applied when the surface of the concrete is moist and in this way prevent evaporation. After the curing period, the asphalt may be peeled off the surface and reused.

3. Calcium chloride in a very rich solution sprinkled on the surface of the pavement as soon as the concrete has taken its final set may also be used with some success. This material has an affinity for drawing moisture from the air, hence when it is used on the surface of a pavement, the pavement is kept moist. The objection to this method is the expense and the possibility of the chloride solution being washed off the surface by a heavy rainfall. A slight covering of earth (½ to 1 inch) in connection with the use of calcium chloride is desirable as it assists in preventing the material from being washed off.

4. The road surface may be kept moist by installing a pipe line down the center of the pavement and inserting spraying nozzles at intervals of from 15 to 25 feet. In a few instances this method of curing has proved satisfactory. However, in general there are always a few of the spraying nozzles that will get out of order and the pressure will vary between the high and low points in the road so that a uniform spray cannot be maintained. Hence the road will not be uniformly cured.

The cost of curing for any of the methods described above will vary from 4 to 12 cents per square yard of surface.

99. *Fall and Spring Curing.* During the early spring and late fall it is not always necessary to cure the pavement by the use of some sort of covering that is kept moist. Pavements finished during the month of April will ordinarily not require any additional moisture or covering to protect them from the sun and wind. However, this should be watched very carefully as we occasionally have hot and windy days during April that make it necessary to protect the pavement at least with two inches of earth. From the first of May until the first of October the pavement should be covered and kept moist to insure proper curing. During October and November it is not usually necessary to add water for curing purposes although it is always advisable to cover the pavement with at least two inches of earth or six or eight inches of straw to protect the surface from frost and freezing.

48

100. *Protecting Surface in Freezing Weather.* In no case sha canvas be laid directly upon concrete before it obtains a set sufficiel to prevent the canvas from marring the surface. In case of a emergency where the road must be covered to protect it from freezin; dry straw may be scattered over the surface of the pavement to sufficient depth to prevent frost or freezing. In general, however, th surface should be dried out by means of artificial heat so that it wi not be marred by the straw or earth covering.

101. *Preventing Concrete from Freezing.* It is possible to pre vent concrete from freezing by adding a small percentage of calciui chloride to the mix. Calcium chloride may be purchased in the pow dered form and added to the mixture in the ratio of two pounds t each one hundred pounds of cement used. This will prevent concret from freezing to a temperature of about 15° F. It is not advisabl to use more than this ratio as it will hasten the setting process t such an extent that it will be impossible for the workmen to finish th pavement. Calcium chloride does not seem to injure the concrete mi in any way, but it causes the concrete to set so quickly that it attair a strength in five or six days almost equal to that of ordinary concret after a period of thirty days. There is objection, however, to the use c calcium chloride in connection with reinforced concrete as it will a' tack and destroy the reinforcing steel. Ordinary salt is used frequentl in concrete to lower the freezing temperature. This should not be use as it is possible to lower the temperature but two or three degrees an this is not sufficient to insure safety. The best method to follow i laying concrete in freezing weather is to heat the materials before mi ing and then to protect the work from freezing until it has set for period of at least five days.

MONOLITHIC BRICK PAVEMENTS.

102. Monolithic brick pavement construction consists principall in laying the brick directly upon the soft concrete base instead of la ing them upon a sand cushion as has been the practice for many year The concrete base for this type of pavement construction shall there fore be very uniform in consistency and slightly dryer than is normall used in concrete road construction. It should, not, however, be so dr that the voids will not readily be filled and the work finished to th desired cross section. The consistency of the concrete should b such as to allow a film of mortar to come to the surface of the cor crete after it has been tamped three or four times.

103. *Finishing Base Course.* If a finishing machine is used o the base it will strike off the surface so that the brick may be lai directly upon the soft concrete. In a few instances where contractor have been unsuccessful in getting a uniformly finished base they hav added a thin covering of 1:3 dry cement and sand. The dry materi: fills up the porous spots and permits a uniform bearing for the bricl In this case the brick shall be laid and tamped before any initial s{ takes place so that sufficient moisture may be drawn from the concret

base to thoroughly saturate the film of dry sand and cement used on the surface. In general, the use of the dry sand and cement film should be discouraged. If the concrete base is properly proportioned, mixed, and finished, the best results will be secured by laying the brick directly upon the concrete.

Fig. 20. Monolithic brick road showing concrete base and brick surface being finished with a mechanical tamping and finishing machine.

104. *Finishing Brick Surface.* As soon as the brick have been laid they shall be carefully culled and then rolled by means of a hand roller weighing not less than 600 pounds. The pavement shall be rolled lengthwise, crosswise, and at a 45-degree angle and all rolling completed before the initial set takes place in the concrete.

Instead of using a hand roller for finishing the brick, a very light tandem steam roller weighing not more than two tons may be used, if such a unit could be secured. In place of the roller an extra finishing machine may be used to finish the brick to the desired cross section. When the finishing machine is used, it should be independent of the machine used on the concrete base and should be operated over the surface a sufficient number of times to insure that all brick are embedded properly and that the surface is made smooth.

105. *Grouting Brick Surface.* After the rolling has been done, the grouting may be delayed until the close of the day. It is necessary, however, to complete each day the grouting for that day's work and not allow the brick to remain open to be grouted the next day. The grouting shall extend up to the header board and when the work starts the following morning the first four or five feet of the base should be finished by hand tamping. Extreme care should be taken at the construction joints to see that the brick are thoroughly imbedded in the soft concrete base and that no irregularities in the surface exist in the finished pavement. The grouting of the brick surface is one of the most essential parts of successful brick road construction.

Extreme care shall be taken to see that the grout penetrates to th full depth of the brick. It usually requires three independent opera tions to thoroughly grout the surface of a brick pavement. The fina grouting shall be squeegeed very carefully and all surplus morta pushed forward. The final squeegee shall be on a 45-degree angl so as not to wipe the mortar out of the joints.

106. *Uniform Surface.* The engineer in charge of brick con struction shall follow all of the suggestions outlined under "Concret Pavements" with respect to securing a uniform surface. The 10-foc straight edge shall be used constantly on the brick surface to see tha the entire pavement is finished within the requirements of the spec: fications.

107. *Curing.* Within a few hours after the brick pavemer has been grouted, it shall be covered with frames, canvas, or othe material to protect it from sun and wind. The specifications requir brick pavements to be cured for a period of ten days. This may b done in the same manner as outlined for curing concrete pavement:

BITUMINOUS FILLED BRICK CONSTRUCTION.

108. *Concrete Base.* The concrete base for bituminous fille brick pavements shall be tamped and finished as required for an oi dinary concrete road.

109. *Curing Base.* The concrete base shall be cured for a pei iod of at least ten days, following the same methods as outlined unde "Concrete Pavements." The base for a bituminous filled brick road wi usually have a monolithic concrete curb. This will be of assistanc when the ponding method is used for curing the pavement. If th ponding method is not used, a straw covering kept wet will probabl prove most satisfactory as this method will permit the base to b cleaned more easily preparatory to laying the cushion and brick.

110. *Gravel and Macadam Bases.* Old gravel or macadai roads may in a few instances be utilized as a base for bituminot filled brick pavement surfaces. If such a base is used it should hav a depth of at least eight inches and a width slightly greater than th width of the finished pavement. The ordinary gravel or macadai road will usually have to be reshaped before laying the brick surfac This can be done by slightly scarifying the surface, adding sufficiei new material and rerolling it to secure the desired cross section.

111. *Cushion.* The cushion may be of sand or limestone dus In the case of a macadam or gravel base the cushion will have to b from one to two inches in thickness to take up the irregularities i the surface and give the desired finish. The cushion on a concret base shall not be thicker than one inch and preferably not more tha three-fourths of an inch. In every case the sand or limestone du: cushion shall be thoroughly compacted so that when it is struck o true to the cross section, the brick will not roll to an uneven finisl In a few instances a mixture of sand and cement in the ratio of 1: has been used as a cushion, and in other cases a mixture of bituminot

material and sand. The object of the cement or bituminous material is to prevent displacement of the cushion during the life of the wearing surface.

112. *Laying and Rolling Brick.* The bituminous filled brick shall be laid, culled and rolled in the usual manner except that the rolling shall be done with a three to five-ton tandem roller. It is practically impossible to roll the road at right angles with a power driven roller, but the surface can be thoroughly rolled longitudinally and at an angle of 45 degrees.

113. *Bituminous Filler.* After the rolling, the pavement shall be carefully culled for broken brick and the surface filled with a bituminous filler. If a sand cement cushion is used it shall be thoroughly saturated with water and allowed to dry out before the pavement is filled. The bituminous filler shall be applied at as high a temperature as is permissible and on days when it is warm and the brick are dry. It may be squeegeed into the brick surface and a light film of material left over the entire surface of the pavement.

114. *Curing Surface.* No curing is necessary for bituminous filled brick pavements and the work may be opened to traffic within about 24 hours after the pavement is finished.

BITUMINOUS CONCRETE PAVEMENTS.

115. *Finishing Base.* The base for bituminous concrete pavements shall be finished with a finishing machine the same as a base for a brick pavement or a concrete road. After being finished and just prior to the initial set of the concrete, the surface shall be rolled with a corrugated hand roller. The rolling shall be done at an angle of about 45 degrees with the road in both directions so that the surface will be roughened to a depth of from one-fourth to three-fourths of

Fig. 21. Corrugated hand roller used to roughen concrete surface for a bituminous concrete pavement.

an inch. The purpose of roughening the surface is to insure a perfec
bond between the bituminous wearing surface and the concrete base

116. *Curing.* The base for bituminous concrete pavements wil
usually have a monolithic concrete curb which will assist in curing
the concrete base if the ponding method is used. If this method
cannot be used it is desirable to cure by the use of a straw covering
as the base may be more readily cleaned before applying the wearing
surface. The curing shall be done very carefully and over a period o·
at least ten days.

Fig. 22. Dumping, spreading, and rolling bituminous concrete on a
concrete base.

117. *Concrete Curb.* The concrete curb on the bituminou:
filled brick pavement and the bituminous concrete pavement may b(
built monolithically by using a special finishing machine that will tam̨
and finish the base to the depth of the curb below the outside forms
A longitudinal retaining strip of angle iron or wood may be set foɪ
the inside forms of the curb and held in place by means of clamp:
which will hook over the outside forms. The space between th(
temporary forms and the outside forms may then be filled with con·
crete and tamped and finished. This can be done within a distanc(
of 40 feet behind the concrete that is being laid in the base. The smal
amount of concrete used in the curbs, therefore, may be carried back
in large shovels or wheeled back in wheel-barrows.

118. *Binder and Wearing Courses.* After the concrete base ha:
been cured for a period of at least ten days and in addition hardenec
for a period of at least twenty days, it may be covered with the bindeɪ
course which shall be followed immediately by the top or wearing
course. The total thickness of the binder and wearing courses doe:
not usually exceed three inches. The binder course is therefore fronͭ
one and one-half to two inches in thickness. The same type anc
weight of tandem roller may be used for both courses. The rolling

n each case shall be done immediately after the material is uniformly
pread and in such a manner that the finished surface will be per-
ectly smooth. The rolling as well as the spreading of the bituminous
oncrete should be done by experienced men to insure a uniform
vearing surface. In no case shall the finished surface deviate more
han one-fourth inch from a ten-foot straight edge.

GRAVEL ROADS.

119. Gravel roads are built either by the trench method or the
eather-edge method. If only a small amount of gravel is to be used
or surfacing or building a road (4 to 6 inches) it preferably should
ie placed according to the feather-edge method. If a greater thick-
ess is to be applied, better results will be obtained by building it accord-
ng to the trench method or at least by constructing it so that the
iase course will be in a trench and the wearing course feather-edged
o the desired width of the improvement. If coarse gravel or a very
arge portion of it has been crushed, it is advisable to follow the trench
onstruction method. This method will permit the surface to be more
horoughly rolled and bonded. If the gravel is fine (1 inch and under)
nd contains a large portion of clay binder, better results will be ob-
ained by following the feather-edge method as it is practically impos-
ible to roll fine material with any success. Gravel roads that are built
ccording to the feather-edge method can usually be compacted by frequently dragging the surface. When fine gravel is used, it is desirable
hat it contain not over 25 per cent of material passing a one-fourth
nch screen and not to exceed 15 per cent of clay binder. Gravel con-
aining less binder may require considerably more time to become com-
iacted under traffic but the road obtained will prove to be much bet-
er after it has once become consolidated.

Fig. 23. Trench method of constructing macadam or gravel roads.

120. *Trench and Feather-edge Construction.* A combination of
he trench and feather-edge methods may be used to an advantage in

certain instances. The bottom part of the gravel road for about tw
thirds the width of the finished pavement may be constructed in accor
ance with the trench method. After the bottom course has been sprea
and thoroughly compacted the entire surface may be shaped and t'
wearing course of three to six inches applied in accordance with tl
feather-edge method. This combination of methods will save a litt
gravel and prove to be very satisfactory.

Fig. 24. Gravel road constructed by the feather-edge method.

121. *Crown.* The crown on a gravel road should not be ov
three inches for an 18-foot width. Excess crown will force traffic
the middle of the road and this will result in unnecessary rutting.
the gravel road is properly maintained, a very light crown will ter
to distribute traffic over the entire surface thereby lengthening the li
of the road. In general, it is advisable to build gravel roads fully :
feet in width for two lines of traffic. By getting a wider surfac
traffic does not become concentrated and the gravel surface will ho
up under less maintenance.

MACADAM ROADS.

122. Macadam roads are usually constructed by following tl
trench method. The stone preferably should be applied in two ind
pendent layers of about five inches in thickness and each layer tho
oughly rolled and bonded with screenings or bonding gravel. Tl
stone should be uniformly graded in size from $1\frac{1}{2}$ to $2\frac{1}{2}$ inches. Tl
roller used shall be a 10-ton, 3-wheeled type. Sufficient rolling sh
be done to key the stone together thoroughly and to prevent its movir
about when walked upon. Either the screenings or bonding grav
shall be washed into the voids of the stone at the time of constructic
or the road shall be kept closed to traffic until there is sufficient rainf
to accomplish this result. The finished surface of a macadam or grav
road shall not deviate more than one-half inch from a 10-foot straigl
edge.

123. *Crown.* The crown on a macadam road shall not exceed ɔur inches for an 18-foot pavement. The small crown will tend to distribute traffic over the entire macadam surface thereby increasing its ɩe very materially.

Macadam roads can be maintained by applying frequently a small mount of bonding gravel or bonding screenings. If the surface is llowed to become bare for lack of bonding material, the stone will soon ecome dislodged causing the surface to begin to ravel.

BITUMINOUS MACADAM ROADS.

124. Bituminous macadam roads are built somewhat similar to rdinary macadam roads except that the top two and one-half or three ɪches of stone are penetrated with bituminous material (from 2 to 2½ allons per square yard) and then choked with stone chips or torpede ravel. The purpose of this filler is to hold the large stone in place nd prevent raveling of the road surface. The method outlined in the pecifications should be followed very carefully in this type of conɩruction.

125. *Surface Treatment.* Many macadam and gravel roads deɩriorate very rapidly under motor driven traffic. To prevent raveling ɩ is necessary continually to apply additional binder to the surface ɩch as screenings or bonding gravel. There is also considerable annoynce on account of the dust rising from gravel and macadam roads. ɩuch surfaces are therefore improved by sweeping off all surplus fine ɩaterial and applying a light application of asphalt or tar and then

Fig. 25. Method used for distributing bituminous material for surface treatment of macadam and gravel roads or for oiling earth roads.

overing the surface with sand or stone chips. A well constructed ɩacadam road may be surface treated with considerable success in this ɩanner and maintained in a condition that is much more desirable than

that of the ordinary macadam road. The surface mat can be main
tained by applying annually a small amount of bituminous materi
and stone chips or torpedo gravel.

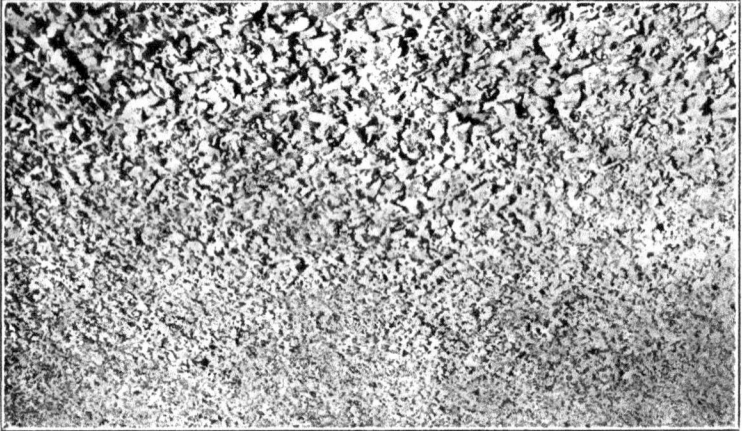

Fig. 26. Condition of macadam surface after first application of one
and one-half to two gallons per square yard of bituminous material is
applied. This treatment to be followed with stone chips or torpedo
gravel then one-half to three-fourths gallon per square yard and another covering of stone chips or gravel.

126. *Surface Treating Gravel Roads.* Very little success h
thus far been attained in the surface treatment of gravel roads
Illinois. The principal reason for this is that most of the grav
roads contain a very large percentage of clay binder and the cl
prevents the bituminous material from properly binding and holdi
the gravel surface. Considerable success has been experienced, hoy
ever in oiling gravel roads which have a moderate traffic but
heavy truck traffic. The paraffin base asphaltic oils having a 40
50 per cent residue may be applied to such roads at the rate of abo
one-half to three-fourths gallon per square yard of surface. The
should be spread in two applications and each covered with sto
chips ranging in size from one-half to three-fourths of an inch. Aft
this light oil has permeated most of the clay binder and the surfa
has formed a fairly good mat, the road may be treated with a bett
grade of asphalt or refined tar and stone chips again applied. Th
method will build up a mat on the surface of a gravel road that w
withstand moderately heavy traffic. This type of construction is d
sirable for secondary roads and streets and particularly roads whi
have considerable pleasure traffic.

EARTH ROADS.

127. Earth roads should be constructed to a width of 24 to
feet exclusive of the ditches. The crown should be from 6 to 12 inch
and if the road is properly maintained, the lighter crown will pro
much more desirable.

128. *Grading Machinery.* Earth roads will ordinarily be constructed by the use of graders having a blade 8 to 12 feet in length which may be pulled by 20 to 40-horse power gas or steam engines. After the heavy grading work has been done, the surface may be shaped and maintained with an ordinary drag, light grader, or leveler. Where it is necessary to move a portion of the earth longitudinally with the road, it can be done by the use of elevating graders discharging directly into dump wagons that will carry the earth to the desired location. In heavy cuts, steam shovels can be used to an advantage. On ordinary work, Maney scrapers, wheel scrapers, fresnoes, or slips may be used to pull the earth from the hills into the low places. After the earth road has been graded so that it will properly drain, the chief problem is that of maintenance.

129. *Earth Road Maintenance.* The earth surface will become very badly rutted and out of shape following each rain. It is therefore necessary to provide for constant maintenance to keep the surface smooth and in a condition that it will shed water. The maintenance can be best handled by the use of the ordinary road drags which may be either of the wood or steel type. In many cases the Minnesota road planer, the leveler, or the three-way drag is used, but most any form of a drag will prove satisfactory. The main object is to keep the surface smooth and to smoothen it at times when the operation is most effective.

OILED EARTH ROADS.

130. Earth roads may be maintained more satisfactorily by one or two applications of road oil each year. Before the road oil is applied, the earth should be shaped to the desired cross section and the surface made smooth and free from dust. The oil should then be applied for a width of about 15 feet at the rate of one-half gallon per square yard of surface. The oil shall be put on in two applications of one-fourth gallon in each application. If considerable time is allowed to elapse between the two treatments, better results will be assured. The road oil for the first application shall contain from 45 to 55 per cent asphaltum residue and shall be applied hot so that it will thoroughly penetrate the earth surface. The second and succeeding applications may be of slightly heavier consistency (50 to 60 per cent residue). In each case the oil shall be heated so that it will thoroughly penetrate the road surface when put on. The first treatment of road oil can ordinarily be spread in April, and the second in June. This will allow the road to go through the major part of the summer free from dust and mud. A fall application in September is sometimes desirable although not always economical. Fall oiling can hardly be justified on account of the expense. The primary object of the oil is to suppress the dust and to prevent mud through the summer and fall months. In general therefore, the oil shall be applied in the spring before the dust forms. On moderately traveled roads, and during some mild winters, the fall oiling may prevent mud throughout the re-

mainder of the year. The average winter in Illinois, however, w
cause the oiled surface to break through under heavy traffic.

Fig. 27. Well graded and oiled earth road.

The oiled surface can be maintained satisfactorily by the u
of a light drag following a rain. An oiled surface that has becor
pitted can be repaired by slightly scarifying the entire surface
the road and thoroughly dragging it during or following a rain.
should then have another light treatment of oil if possible. T
cause of most pit holes in the oiled surface is that the road surface do
not absorb the oil when it is first applied.

SHOULDERS AND SIDE DITCHES.

131. *Cross Section.* Properly shaped shoulders and side ditch
add materially to the life of an improved road as well as to its a
pearance. Earth shoulders shall be graded to a uniform width fro
the edge of the pavement and sloped sufficiently to drain the surfa
water to the side ditches readily. When earth shoulders are first co
structed of loose material, it is desirable to build them practically le\
to their full width. After the earth has become settled they will \
ually have the slope necessary to carry off surface water. If t
shoulders could be thoroughly rolled or compacted during constructi
they could be built to the standard slope shown on the plans but tl
is practically impossible, hence they must be built up level and \
lowed to settle to the desired slope.

132. *Side Ditches.* The side ditches preferably should be ma
by the use of a slip scraper or a specially designed grader blade. T
back slope on the side ditches should be made by the use of a sm
grader that will throw some of the material towards the fence line. /
abrupt bank on the back slope shall not be allowed as this mater
will easily cave and fill the ditches.

133. *Hand Work.* Extreme care shall be exercised in gradi
the ditches to make certain they will drain to the outlets in the ro\

t is not necessary to require hand work on the shoulders, side ditches, or back slopes provided the contractor is capable of getting satisfactory results by the use of machines. On deep cuts, however, it may frequently be desirable to do a small amount of hand work to prevent unnecessary sloughing of the loose materials into the side ditches.

Fig. 28. Showing well shaped shoulder and side ditch.

134. *Finisihng Shoulders.* Shoulders, side ditches, and back slopes shall be finished complete just as soon as the pavement is ready to be opened to traffic. Delay in finishing the shoulders and ditches may cause serious accidents when the road is opened to traffic, and may further cause considerable delay in final payment to the contractor on account of the work not being completed and ready for final acceptance. As soon as the grading has been completed to the desired cross section, the shoulders shall be seeded in accordance with the specifications to prevent unnecessary erosion.

135. *Entrance Culverts.* All farm entrance culverts shall be built after the shoulders and side ditches have been formed with the grading machine. If the culverts are constructed in advance they are frequently out of alignment and not built to the grade of the ditch line. If this practice is followed, the contractor will be required to do considerable hand work adjacent to the culverts to properly shape the shoulders and ditches and thus add to the cost of his work.

ACCEPTANCE OF WORK.

136. A road is ready for final acceptance when the shoulders, side ditches, and back slopes have been properly finished and seeded, and all incidental work in connection with the pavement is completed in accordance with the plans and specifications.

137. *Completing Details of Work.* The specifications stipulate that immediately upon the satisfactory completion of a section of road,

and upon the written approval of same by the engineer, the contract
shall be relieved of any requirements for further work on such se
tion. It is therefore suggested that contractors complete all details
their work as they go to permit a partial acceptance and full payme
on the completed portion. In a great many cases final payment (
both a partial acceptance and a final acceptance has been withheld (
account of minor work remaining undone, the value of which ma
amount to but a few hundred dollars. Such negligence on the part (
the contractor, therefore, seriously ties up considerable money that ma
be due him.

138. *Certified Checks.* In a few instances where only a sma
amount of work remains to be done to secure final acceptance, cert
fied checks have been accepted in lieu of unfinished work. This pra
tice, however, will not be tolerated except in instances where the co
tractor shows sufficient evidence that he has not been able to comple
the small details of his work for causes beyond his control. Whc
certified checks are submitted they shall not exceed approximately $5(
for the section of work under consideration for acceptance.

139. *Partial Acceptance..* In the case of a partial acceptance (
a section, it should be kept in mind that the Department cannot acce
any portion of a contract unless the portion finished is approximate
one mile in length and will become of some service to the travelir
public when accepted and opened for use.

PAYMENT ESTIMATES.

140. The district engineer shall submit to the Division of Higl
ways, Bureau of Construction, not oftener than twice each month a
estimate in triplicate of the work completed by the contractor on whic
the contractor shall be paid 90 per cent of the estimate, the remainir
10 per cent to be held in reserve until the completion and acceptanc
of the entire work.

The following instructions shall be followed in making out pa;
ment estimates:

1. Payment estimates shall be made up from the contrac
and not from the project agreement of the section under cor
sideration.

2. All estimates shall show quantities completed to dat
including extras and in all cases the completed quantities mult
plied by the unit prices shall equal the amount shown in th
"Value Completed" column.

3. All estimates, except semi-final estimates, shall show th
total quantities as awarded.

4. All estimates, except semi-final estimates, shall show th
total quantities added or deducted opposite the corresponding iter
of work.

5. The value of extras and deductions shall be shown in th
proper columns but added or subtracted as the case may b
to the total value of the contract. Additions or deductions affec
the contract price and the total amount eventually due.

6. The total value of each item as awarded need not be shown except in the final estimate.

7. Allowances for materials in storage shall be shown in the Payment Estimate record. Materials stored shall be on the cumulative basis and shall show in the respective columns the quantity of material received, used, and on hand. Requests for reimbursement for materials stored shall be accompanied by the receipted bills or itemized statement and affidavit as outlined in "Payment for Materials."

8. Allowances for excess freight and war tax shall be shown under "Miscellaneous Credits." Such allowances shall also be accompanied by an itemized statement and affidavit as outlined in "Freight Increases and Reductions."

9. The 10 per cent retention shall not be made from materials in storage or from excess freight or war tax.

10. No allowances shall be included in semi-final estimates for materials stored or for excess freight and war tax.

11. Make a regular engineer's payment estimate covering the portion of the work under consideration before a semi-final estimate is made. Semi-final estimates shall be made on the same form as the regular monthly estimates.

12. Attach to the final estimate an itemized list of all cement shipments received since the previous estimates.

13. With semi-final and final estimates submit final inspection report, affidavit, and bills for all miscellaneous extra work. With semi-final estimates a release from the bonding company shall be submitted as outlined under "Semi-final Estimates."

14. When inspectors submit monthly estimates to the district engineer, they shall be accompanied by a letter of explanation showing how the quantities on the estimate were arrived at.

141. *Payment for Materials.* The Department may at its discretion pay for any or all materials purchased and delivered f. o. b. the railroad siding provided such material meets the requirements of the district engineer. The amount thus paid, however, shall go to reduce estimates to the contractor as the material is used in the work. If the contractor desires to ask for payment on such materials he shall submit to the engineer the receipted material bills in triplicate, or, if he desires to retain the bills he may submit an itemized statement of the bills together with an affidavit (similar to Fig. 29, Form M-88) certifying to the quantity and cost of the material f. o. b. the railroad siding. On contracts awarded under the 1919 specifications, it is necessary to have a release from the contractor's bondsman granting permission to the State Division of Highways to pay for materials delivered. Such release or supplementary agreement is to be attached to the contract on file in the main office. The blank form of release should be obtained from the Springfield office and sent in previous to the forwarding of the estimates in order to have them approved and signed by the Department in advance of the time the estimate is received so that payment for the work will not be delayed. The 1920

and 1921 specifications provide for payment of materials, therefor no release is required.

142. *Freight Increases and Reductions.* In accordance with th specifications, contractors will be allowed all increases in freigh effective from the date of the receipt of bids. Contractors makin claim for payment of increased freight shall submit on Fig. 30 a itemized statement of the cars received on which reimbursement i requested. He shall also submit published tariff rates or sufficier evidence to show the rate in effect on the date of the bids and th rate and date of the various increases. The itemized statement sha be accompanied by an affidavit, similar to Fig. 31.

In case a reduction in freight is made, similar forms shall be usec

143. *Semi-final Estimates.* When a portion of a section in specific contract is entirely completed and ready for acceptance, th district engineer may submit to the Springfield office a semi-final est: mate which will allow the 10 per cent that has been withheld in prev ious estimates on the completed work. Semi-final estimates shall als be accompanied by a final inspection report by the district enginee and an affidavit from the contractor certifying that all sums of mone due for labor, material, machinery, etc. have been paid. A releas from the bonding company authorizing payment in full for the por tion completed shall be mailed to the main office before payments ca be made on a semi-final estimate. This release shall be submitted o Fig. 32, Form M-62.

144. *Affidavit.* When an entire road or a portion of a road i ready for final acceptance, all money due the contractor shall be pai him provided he will furnish an affidavit similar to Fig. 33. Form 14 showing that all sums of money due for labor, material, apparatus, fix tures, or machinery furnished for the improvement in question hav been paid, or that the person to whom money may be due consents t final payment being made to the contractor.

FORM OF STATEMENT AND AFFIDAVIT FOR MATERIAL STORED.

The following form should be followed by all contractors who ex pect reimbursements on materials placed in storage.

ITEMIZED MATERIAL STATEMENT.

Materials received from................192.... to...................192.... are as follows

................tons of Gravel @ .... per ton f. o. b............................ = ...
                                                      shipping point

.... " " Sand @ .... " " " .... = ...
                                                      shipping point

.... " " Stone @ .... " " " .... = ...
                                                      shipping point
                                                               Total = ...

FREIGHT.

.... " " Gravel @ .... " " " ....
destination

.... " " Sand @ .... " " " ....
destination

.... " " Stone @ .... " " " ....
destination

Total ....

Grand total ....

Approved..Contractor.

....Resident Engineer or District Engineer

STATE OF ILLINOIS, }
County of................................ } ss.

AFFIDAVIT.

Mr...being first duly sworn, deposes

and says that he represents the...Company
and is authorized to make the following statement:

That the above named materials (or materials listed on attached statement) have been received and stored, to the satisfaction of the representa-
ive of the State Division of Highways for use in the construction of Section

........................Project ....Route ....

That the sum of $........................has been paid the........................

R. R. for freight on said material and that the sum of $........................

has been paid the........................Company for said materials

f. o. b........................

Further, that this affidavit is made for the purpose of obtaining payment on said materials in accordance with supplementary contract dated

........................and supplementary letter by the Department of Public Works and Buildings dated January 22, 1920.

....
Contractor.

By........................

Subscribed and sworn to before me this........................day of

........................192......

(Notary Seal)

....
Notary Public

Note: The above affidavit shall be made on the itemized bill or attached
to the statement submitted.

Fig. 29

Form M-88

MEMORANDUM OF CARS RECEIVED.

Section.................... , ...County, Proj. or Route ....

Kind of material......................... From whom purchased.............. ....

Shipping Point...................................., Name of R. R................................

Published tariff rate........................... Date on which increase or reduction

became effective.. .

Date shipped.	Car initial and number.	Capacity.	Freight rate.	Value.	Amount of war tax.	Amount of 10c Frt.	Amount of increase or reduction.

Keep sand, stone, steel, etc. separate giving the company and railroad over which material was shipped.

List cars according to dates so that each list will show the complete number of cars received during any particular interval.

Make the statement in triplicate. Attach affidavits to lists and mail to district engineer.

Engineer's O. K. and railroad agent's approval, when possible to secure it, should be shown on each statement.

O. K.. ....

Resident Engineer   Contractor

....

District Engineer   R. R. Agent

FIG. 30.

State of Illinois
County of.................... } ss.

AFFIDAVIT.

Mr...being first duly sworn,

deposes and says that he represents the...

....Company and is authorized to make the
following statement.

That the above named materials (or materials listed on attached statement) have been received and the war tax and freight as indicated have

been paid for materials used in the construction of Section..........................,

Project..................., Bond Issue Route...........................

Further, that this affidavit is made for the purpose of obtaining refund
from the State for war tax; the 10-cent reduction in freight which the contractor was supposed to receive on road building material and all increases
in freight rate since the date of the contract and particularly since August

26, 1920 in accordance with contract dated..

....

....
Contractor.

By..

Subscribed and sworn to before me this..

day of...192.........

[NOTARY SEAL.]

....
Notary Public.

FIG. 31...................

RELEASE FOR SEMI-FINAL ESTIMATE.

The Department of Public Works and Buildings is hereby authorized
and requested to make payment in full to the contractor upon contract

named below for such portion of the same as may be completed by...................

....and approved by the Chief Highway
Engineer, or his duly authorized representative.

This authorization to be attached to our bond issued to the Department

of Public Works and Buildings covering the contract of.......................................

for Project..................., Section....................in.......................................

....County, and is to become a part of said surety
contract.

....

By..

FIG. 32, FORM M-62.

STATE OF ILLINOIS

COUNTY OF... } ss.

CONTRACTOR'S AFFIDAVIT.

....

having completed the improvement of a..aid

road known as Section................................, ...

County, Project................., Route................., in accordance with the plans

specifications, proposal and bid relating thereto, as provided for in contrac

approved...192........., being duly

sworn on oath, doth say that all sums of money due for any labor, material

apparatus, fixtures or machinery used in such construction, and that al

damages, direct or indirect, suffered or claimed on account of such con

struction or improvement, have been paid.

....

By..

Subscribed and sworn to before me this...day

of..192......... .

....

Notary Public.

FIG. 33.   FORM No. 141.

(SUGGESTED FORM OF BILL FOR EXTRA WORK.)

Department of Public Works and Buildings
Division of Highways, Dr.

to

Contractor.

Contractor.

Examined and found correct:

Resident or District Engineer.

FIG. 34.

DETOUR AND BARRICADE SIGNS.

145. All detour, slow and barricade signs shall be erected and maintained by the engineer in charge of the road or bridge being improved. All signs necessary to guide the traveling public around any highway that has been closed for improvement shall be secured from your district engineer.

All signs erected shall be securely fastened to a solid background by means of paste or tacking completely around the margin at intervals of not more than three inches. If thin paper signs are supplied they may be pasted to a board background, if the heavy cardboard sign is supplied it will have been dipped in paraffin or shellac to protect it from the action of the weather.

146. *Slow Sign.* The slow sign, (Fig. 35) shall be erected on a post set in the outer edge of the shoulder about 400 feet ahead of the barricade. The top of the sign shall be about 4 feet from the ground line, the post supporting the sign shall not be smaller than a 2 x 4 and shall be set at least 2 feet into the ground.

147. *Road Closed.* The road closed sign, (Fig. 36) shall be erected on two substantial posts set in front but independent of the barricade. The posts shall be at least 2″ x 4″ x 7′ long and set two feet apart and at least two feet into the ground at a point where they will not be disturbed by traffic. On the "Road Closed" sign you shall print carefully sufficient information to guide the traveling public around the road that is closed for improvement, ie. N-2 mi; W-3 mi; S-2 mi brings you back onto the road.

148. *Detour signs.* A detour sign shall be fastened immediately below the "Road Closed" sign, with its arrow pointing in the direction of the detour. Detour signs shall be erected in such way that traffic going in both directions may readily follow the detour. There shall be at least two signs at all cross or intersecting roads and a sign along the road at least every mile. If existing poles are not located in position desired substantial posts shall be securely set at the desired points and the "Detour" signs securely nailed to them. The post shall be set so that the traffic that is being detoured may readily see the sign and not fail to make the proper turn. Figure 38 will serve as a guide in the location of the different signs.

149. *Purchasing and erecting.* Unless otherwise instructed by your district engineer you will make a memorandum of the sign boards and posts needed to detour the work at all times during its construction. You will then go to the nearest lumber yard and secure sufficient lumber for the signs needed and get a receipted bill, which you may turn in at the same time you forward your expense account. The contractor will probably loan you the necessary tools to make and erect the signs. If extra help is needed hire a man and get a receipt for the amount paid.

150. *Maintenance of Signs.* From time to time determine the signs that are actually needed to detour the traffic around that portion of the road that is closed. Try and check all signs each day or at

least twice each week to see that they are in place. No excuse will be accepted for not having all signs erected and maintained in such way that inconvenience to the traveling public will be minimized.

151. *Maintenance of detour road.* If the road on which you have chosen to detour traffic is in need of dragging or maintenance, get in touch with the local township commissioner and exert your influence to have the road dragged. It might be well to determine your detours as soon as you arrive on the job and consult the highway commissioner concerning their maintenance. This will give the commissioner a more active interest in the construction of the road and will result in his cooperation from the start.

BARRICADES.

152. It is the duty of the engineer to see that the contractor puts up proper barricades, maintains them during construction and completely removes them from the site before final acceptance.

Barricades should be constructed in the following manner: Posts shall be erected at 5' centers entirely across the roadway and at least one line of 2" x 6" timber spiked near the top of the posts. The posts shall be 6" x 7' long, of sound material and set at least 3' into the ground. In case it is necessary to permit people living along the road entrance through the barricade, opening shall be provided, preferably near the center of the roadway and a substantial gate erected. The entire barricade shall then be whitewashed or painted white. The contractor shall be required to see that the barricades are locked and that proper individuals are supplied with keys until the final completion of the road. The contractor may arrange with each property owner living along the road to provide his own key and padlock which may be attached to the gate. When this arrangement is made each padlock forms a link of the locking chain. If the barricade is to remain for any considerable length of time, such as through a winter, it shall be painted with black stripes.

ROAD CLOSED

BY ORDER OF—

CLIFFORD OLDER, *CHIEF HIGHWAY ENGINEER*

VIOLATORS SUBJECT TO ARREST

PENALTY: FINE, IMPRISONMENT OR BOTH

OPEN ONLY TO RESIDENT AND CONTRACTOR'S TRAFFIC

FOLLOW MARKED DETOUR

Engineer in Charge Will Indicate Exact Routing of Detour Giving Mileage and Direction

Road Closed Sign as furnished by Department.

ROAD CLOSED

BY ORDER OF—

CLIFFORD OLDER, *CHIEF HIGHWAY ENGINEER*

VIOLATORS SUBJECT TO ARREST

PENALTY: FINE, IMPRISONMENT OR BOTH

OPEN ONLY TO RESIDENT AND CONTRACTOR'S TRAFFIC

FOLLOW MARKED DETOUR

West 2 mi. South 2 mi. East 2 mi. back to Main Road

Engineer In Charge will Indicate Exact Routing of Detour Giving Mileage and Direction

Road Closed Sign showing Engineers notations.

Fig. 35.

SLOW

BARRICADE - 400FT

STANDARD WARNING SIGN FOR BARRICADES

Fig. 36.

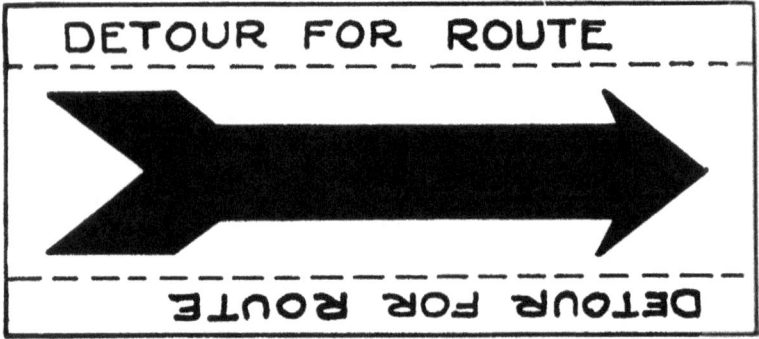

STANDARD DETOUR SIGN AS FURNISHED BY DEPARTMENT

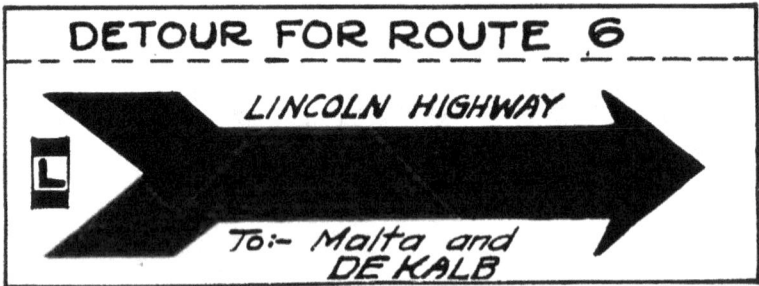

STANDARD DETOUR SIGN SHOWING ENGINEER'S
NOTATIONS BEFORE ERECTING

NOTE—Engineer in charge will indicate before erecting the sign, the Route number, name of Trail, its Emblem if the road has a name and emblem, the next town and County Seat or main City on the road.

Fig. 37.

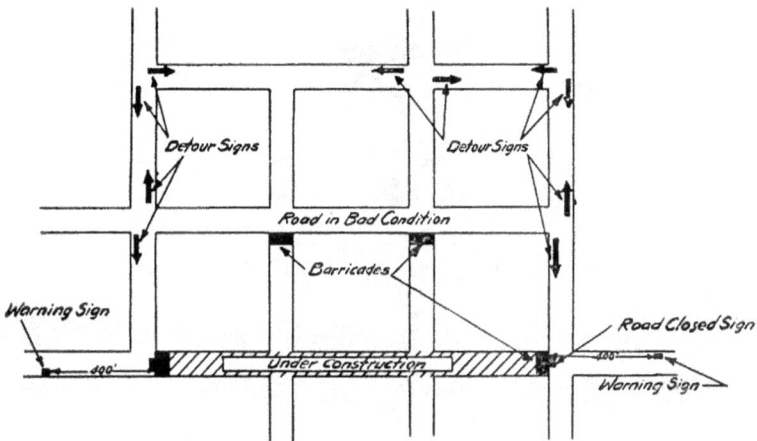

Map showing Position of Barricade and Detour Signs.

Fig. 38.

www.ingramcontent.com/pod-product-compliance
Lightning Source LLC
Chambersburg PA
CBHW052106270326
41931CB00012B/2907